MARKUS SCHIRNER

THE COMPLETE

SMUDGING HANDBOOK

67 Herbs, Woods, and Resins for Clearing and Emotional Balance

EARTHDANCER

AN INNER TRADITIONS IMPRINT

DISCLAIMER The author and publishers accept no liability for the recipes and methods described in this book or for any damages that may arise from using the tips and advice given in this book. Consult your doctor or alternative practitioner in the event of any health concerns. The methods described do not represent an alternative to therapeutic or medicinal treatment.

First edition 2025
The Complete Smudging Handbook
67 Herbs, Woods, and Resins for Clearing and Emotional Balance
Markus Schirner

This English edition © 2025 Earthdancer GmbH
English translation © 2025 JMS books LLP
Editing by JMS books LLP (www.jmseditorial.com)

Originally published in German as *Leitfaden Räuchern mit Harzen, Kräutern und Hölzern – Die besten Praxis-Tipps für Einsteiger*
World © 2022 Schirner Verlag, Darmstadt, Germany

All rights reserved. No part of this book may be reprinted or reproduced or utilized in any form or by any electronic, mechanical, or other means, now known or hereafter invented, including photocopying and recording, or in any information storage or retrieval system, without permission in writing from the publisher.

Cover design: Aaron Davis and Design Is Identity
Cover illustration: Pam Walker/shutterstock.com
Layout by Anna Katharina Berg, Schirner
Typesetting: Chris Bell, cbdesign
Typeset in Minion Pro

Printed and bound in China by Reliance Printing Co., Ltd.

Cataloging-in-Publication Data for this title is available from the Library of Congress.

ISBN 979-8-88850-283-9 (print)
ISBN 979-8-88850-284-6 (ebook)

Published by Earthdancer, an imprint of Inner Traditions
www.earthdancerbooks.com, www.innertraditions.com

Contents

Preface 6
Introduction 7
Smudging Methods 9
The Smudging Ritual 16
Sourcing Smudging Materials 18

The Uses of Smudging 23

Acceptance 24	Grounding 62
Ancestors 26	Headaches 65
Annual Festivals 28	Healing 66
Blessing and Consecration 33	Insect Repellent 69
Clarity 36	Letting Go 69
Cleansing 38	Light-Bringers 72
Concentration 44	Love and Sensuality 73
Courage and Self-Confidence 47	Meditation and Inner Vision 77
Creativity and Inspiration 48	Muscle Tension and Stiffness 78
Divination and Clairvoyance 49	New Beginnings and Transition 79
Dreams 52	The Nights of Yuletide 82
Energy and Vitality 53	Parting 85
Evening Smudging Sessions 55	Prayer and Invocation 88
Fear and Anxiety 57	Protection 89
Good Mood and Joy in Life 59	Respiratory Problems 92
	Rheumatism 94
	Stress and Tension 95
Grief and End-of-Life Care .. 61	Women's Issues 97

Glossary of Herbs & Resins 101

Agarwood	102	Larch	138
Amber	103	Lavender	139
Angelica	104	Lemon Balm	140
Aniseed/Star Anise	105	Marigold	141
Ash	106	Mastic	142
Bay Leaf	107	Meadowsweet (Mead Wort)	143
Benzoin	108	Mistletoe	144
Birch	109	Mugwort	146
Calamus	110	Myrrh	147
Camphor	111	Myrtle	148
Cardamom	112	Nutmeg/Mace	149
Cedar	113	Oak	150
Cedar (American)	114	Opoponax Myrrh	151
Chamomile	115	Palo Santo	152
Cinnamon	116	Patchouli	153
Cloves	117	Peppermint/Mint	154
Copal	118	Rose	155
Cypress	119	Rosemary	156
Dammar Gum	120	Sage	157
Dragon's Blood	121	Sage (White)	158
Elder	122	Sandalwood (Red)	159
Elecampane	124	Sandalwood (White)	160
Elemi	125	Scots Pine	161
Eucalyptus	126	Spikenard	162
Frankincense	127	Spruce	163
Galangal	129	St John's Wort	164
Galbanum	130	Styrax	165
Guggul	131	Sweetgrass/Vernal Grass	166
Hops	132	Thyme	167
Hyssop	133	Tonka	168
Iris	134	Verbena	169
Juniper	135	Vetiver	171
Labdanum	136	Yarrow	172
Lady's Mantle	137		

Epilogue 174
About the Author 175
Picture Credits 176

Preface

ALONG WITH THE USE of essential oils in aromatherapy, the practice of smudging has long fascinated me, a tradition that has been maintained for thousands of years, since human beings first discovered fire and how to use it for their own purposes.

In ancient cultures, the smoke generated in smudging was used to create moods, arouse emotions, invoke gods, and perform various rituals. It was traditionally practiced in the days leading up to Christmas as a way of bidding farewell to the old year and preparing for the new.

Incense is still being used as a means of cleansing today since it brings many benefits, including banishing old, negative energies from a room, keeping pathogens and germs in check, and helping to prevent infection. Incense is also traditionally burned during rituals and ceremonies of dedication and protection. Many of these almost forgotten traditions are flourishing again once more. People are returning to tried-and-trusted practices in order to relax and switch off from the stresses and strains of everyday life. They are looking for a way to exert a positive influence on their feelings, moods, and emotions in order to achieve peace and inner calm, to connect with the elemental power of nature, or simply to relax and indulge in enjoyment of the pleasant fragrance.

Explore the world of incense, learn about its effects, the various ways it can be used, and experience the pleasure of smudging with herbs and resin.

Markus Schirner

Introduction

> Did you know that smudging
>
> - affects the limbic system and influences the emotions?
> - relaxes the mind and soul, promoting inner peace?
> - disinfects and purifies the air in a room?
> - can be used for spiritual cleansing?
> - transforms negative into positive energies?
> - cleanses the aura?
> - can promote concentration and clarity?
> - eases sorrow, pain, and fear?
> - can purge and positively influence the ambience of a room?
> - has symbolic protective powers?
> - helps to ward off flies and mosquitoes?

IF YOU ANSWERED NO to any of these questions, you've come to the right place. There is an incense or herb suitable for use in smudging to cater to every item on this list, whether commonplace or more exotic.

Whether you are an absolute beginner and are exploring smudging for the first time or already have some experience, this book aims to answer all the essential questions, providing inspiration and taking you on a journey through the world of smudging. After looking at the How (How does smudging actually work?) and the What (What incense substances are available?), we shall also look at the Why of smudging (Why use smudging—what can it help to promote or ease?).

In general, we can say that smudging works in three ways:

- On a **physical level**, it has a healing effect. The heat generated releases from the plant active ingredients and volatile oils that can directly influence us physically; for example, by producing an antibacterial, anti-inflammatory, or mood-enhancing effect.

- On an **emotional level**, the scents of incense may affect the limbic system, which regulates our emotions, motivations, and memories, among other processes and functions. Odors are directly linked with memories, which in turn are connected with the emotions provoked by memories. The burning of incense in smudging allows these emotions to be recalled consciously.

- On an **energetic level**, burning incense helps us to release the essence of the original plant (its energetic information and everything that we associate with it), thereby activating its vibration within us.

Smudging also works on its own terms, providing a break in our daily routine, a moment in which we can find stillness by fully focusing on the process itself. These effects can be enhanced by incorporating smudging into a ritual and setting an intention. See Uses of Smudging (p. 23) for rituals that can be adapted as required.

To begin, however, I would like to introduce you to the equipment you need and to explain how to carry out a smudging session.

Smudging Methods

There are various ways to burn incense but the simplest and most convenient is in the form of sticks, cones, candles, or spirals. The incense is ground down and processed into one of these easy-to-use forms. The incense is combined with flammable substances so that it smolders evenly once lit without producing too much smoke. All that is required is a suitable holder and a fireproof base in which to catch the ash.

Incense sticks

The methods used to make incense sticks using a range of ingredients varies from country to country. In India and China, incense sticks are made by applying incense to a thin strip of bamboo or wood, while in Japan and Tibet, high-quality herbs are rolled by hand into the form of sticks. Always be sure to buy good-quality incense since even if you are not consciously aware of it, you will automatically be inhaling some of the smoke when the incense is burned. Even a small amount of smoke can have a subtle effect on your feelings and well-being, so natural and/or organic incense containing no pollutants are ideal.

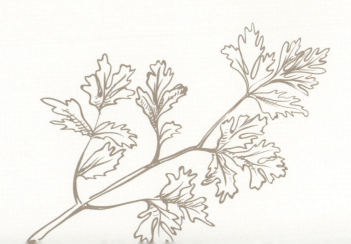

Place the incense sticks in a special holder or a container filled with sand so they can burn right down to the base without any problems.

Incense cones

Incense cones are an alternative to incense sticks. They are usually handmade and are similar to incense sticks in their composition and scent.

Place the cones in a dish, ideally one that contains a layer of sand or salt to insulate the base of the dish and protect the table or surface on which it stands as the cones can become very hot.

Incense cones do not need to be store-bought, they can also be made at home. Begin by making a starch paste to act as an adhesive or binding agent. Mix a little cornstarch with water to form a thick paste and then heat it (warm in a pan on a hob while stirring for around 1 minute). Gum arabic can also be used in place of starch. Allow the binding agent to cool, then add three parts incense mixture (a combination of powdered herbs, wood, and resin to one part cooled binding agent. At least one resin should be included in the incense mixture. For self-combusting cones, add ground charcoal to the mixture as an accelerant. The rule of thumb is approximately 50g charcoal to 10g incense mixture or 60% charcoal/25% incense mixture/15% binding agent.

Small loose pellets of incense can also be made by kneading together ground or crushed herbs with a little mastic powder and a soft gum resin such as labdanum or copaiba balsam. They should be burned on charcoal or an incense burner equipped with a metal mesh.

For something a little special, try incense balls made from sultanas soaked in wine (or mead) and honey (or date syrup) such as Egyptian *kyphi*—recipes are available online and in books, or improvise with your own recipe.

Incense spirals

Incense spirals are made in a similar way to incense sticks but have the advantage of burning for a long time and so are useful for extended rituals or can be used for more than one session. Unlike incense sticks, they burn horizontally and can be extinguished by moistening two fingers and pinching out the part that is alight. This type of incense originated in Japan.

Smudge sticks

Most people are familiar with smudge sticks (or incense bundles) from their association with the indigenous inhabitants of North America, who generally make them from white sage (p. 158) or the tips of the shoots of the American cedar (p. 114). Sweetgrass (p. 166) is generally burned on its own, woven into a tight braid and can be used just like a smudge stick. The advantage of smudge sticks is that they can be burned without charcoal; simply light the stick, put out the flame, and leave the stick to smolder. As a whole stick is rarely burned in one session, it can be extinguished by placing the smoldering tip in sand or soil.

To make a smudge stick, gather together the stems of the fresh herbs being used into a small bunch, then fold the heads of the herbs over and down before tying the bundle together with natural yarn (cotton, linen, hemp) along its whole length. Be sure to tie the bundle tightly enough to be compact, while still being loose enough to allow the herbs to dry out thoroughly and prevent mold from forming inside. Hang the completed smudge stick upside down in a warm, dry, preferably dark place for at least two weeks. Just as with loose incense, smudge sticks should be thoroughly dried before being used, otherwise they may produce thick smoke when burned.

Ordinary domestic kitchen herbs are ideal for making smudge sticks. All herbs in which the whole plant, not just the flower, is burned are suitable. Examples include mugwort, sage, thyme, rosemary, yarrow, mullein, and St John's wort. Herbs that flower at the same time are typically used, for instance, those that flower at the time of the solstice.

Lavender smells very good in smudge sticks, although the flowers have a tendency to explode when heated, which can leave burns or scorch marks on carpets, furniture, clothing, or even skin. Lavender should therefore be packed in the middle of the bundle or alternatively only the lavender leaves should be used.

Smudging with loose herbs

To make smudging more of a celebration and burn homemade rather than store-bought sticks, and especially if you like to choose and assemble your own mixtures, various options for using loose herbs are available.

In addition to the smudging ingredients, you will need a **pair of tongs** or **large pair of tweezers** to safely move burning herbs around on a mesh or plate and to remove the ash of burned incense materials, as well as a **spoon** with which to place the ingredients on the charcoal (see below).

A **feather** can also be useful to guide and waft smoke in the desired direction. Make sure feathers are not sourced from a protected species. Try asking for any shed feathers at a wildlife reserve. The rules are strict with regard to possessing bird feathers, even those that have been shed naturally and can be found in the countryside or garden. Information is available online. Instead of a feather, a fan or piece of stiff paper or card can also be used.

Smudging on charcoal

This is the oldest and most common form of smudging, although the process is a little more involved than others; it is explained in further detail on p. 16.

For smudging on charcoal, you will need a pair of **tongs or tweezers** with which to pick up the hot charcoal safely and a **heat-resistant bowl** or other vessel (such as a brass bowl, a mother-of-pearl shell, or a ceramic dish). Half-fill the vessel with **sand** (quartz sand, sharp sand, or sandbox sand, but note that bird cage sand is not suitable as it contains artificial additives) or **salt**. The sand insulates the bowl from the heat and protects it from the burned (and sometimes sticky) residue left by the herbs; it also allows more air to circulate to the charcoal. Some specialist incense bowls have a thick base or are raised on small legs to protect the surface on which they stand from the heat. Nevertheless, it is still a good idea to place the bowl on a **non-flammable base**. Be careful also not to position the bowl near any soft furnishings that could catch light, and keep animals well away.

Smudging using an incense burner

A good alternative to charcoal that is also a gentler option is to use an incense burner equipped with a metal mesh. Here, the herbs are burned over a gentle flame and don't generate so much smoke.

The substances to be smudged are placed on the metal **mesh** and smolder slowly over a **tea light**. Depending on whether the incense material is placed in the center of the mesh, directly over the flame, or around the edges of the mesh affects the degree of heat to which it is exposed and therefore also the fragrances, which develop differently as a result.

Be careful, as the mesh will become very hot. With resins in particular, which can liquefy, it is a good idea to place a thin layer of **sand** on the mesh to prevent hot resin dripping through. Another option is to use a plate made from fire-resistant material, such as metal or ceramic. Ash can be swept away from the mesh or plate with a feather, or removed with a pair of tweezers or a spoon. If the mesh becomes dirty, wait until it has cooled down and then clean it thoroughly with a brush and some detergent.

Smudging using an essential oil diffuser

This is another gentle smudging method.

Fill the bowl of an **essential oil heat diffuser** with water and light the **tea light** beneath it. As soon as the water starts to steam slightly, add to it the herbs or a few grains of resin. As the heat created by a tea light is considerably less than when burning charcoal, it is a good idea to make sure the herbs are cut into small pieces and that any resins have been first ground down in a mortar. Ground resin can also be mixed with a little **sand**. Both combine when the resin liquifies and release the fragrances into the air more slowly.

Questions and Answers

Question: Could I use a breakfast bowl for smudging?

Answer: Any bowl made of heat-resistant material can be used; for example, ceramic, porcelain, heat-resistant glass (laboratory glassware), or metal. Normal glass is not suitable as the uneven distribution of heat can cause it to crack. Adding an insulating layer of sand to the bowl and placing it on a fire-proof base is always recommended.

Question: Can I use normal barbecue or wood charcoal instead of special charcoal?

Answer: Yes and no. It takes a little more patience for the normal charcoal to catch fire and reach the required heat, but on the other hand, barbecue charcoal has no smell of its own, unlike the charcoal used for smudging which has an accelerant. The special charcoal discs or tablets used for smudging do not get as hot as normal charcoal and glow, keeping their heat, for around 30 to 45 minutes, whereas barbecue charcoal can become so hot that incense ingredients can scorch and burn rather than simply smolder with the heat. A bed of sand can be useful. The flattened shape of the special charcoal discs or tablets is another advantage, with a pre-fabricated hollow to hold the smudging materials.

Question: Can I use earth in place of sand?

Answer: No, this is not recommended; earth often contains organic materials of varying size that may begin to carbonize.

The Smudging Ritual

It is important not to rush a smudging ritual—be sure to allow yourself enough time and space. Precious, high-quality substances are unlocked, transformed, and released into a room when herbs and resins are burned. As the scent is taken in via the body's olfactory system, it is relayed directly to the brain's limbic system, which controls our emotions. Here, a range of different neuromodulators are generated that can modify our mood, our sense of our body, and even our creativity and intuition. As we become more intuitive and less conscious of our reasoned thoughts, everyday life fades into the background, making us more sensitive to subtle energies and open to connecting with higher spheres.

The following example uses a bowl or similar vessel (p. 13). To begin, using a pair of tongs, take a piece of charcoal and hold it over the flame of a candle or a lighter. Charcoal discs and tablets for smudging contain potassium nitrate which acts as an accelerant and creates tiny sparks. Once the charcoal has begun to smoke and crackle softly, place it upright on the sand in the smudging bowl; it takes around five to seven minutes for the charcoal to reach the correct heat, indicated when it turns from a glowing red to white. The charcoal can then be turned over, with the small hollow facing upward. Use a spoon to sprinkle the incense ingredients into the hollow. Start with a small amount and add more as necessary. As a guide, sprinkle as much as you can pinch with three fingers (thumb, index, middle finger). It's a good idea to first cover the charcoal with a thin layer of sand so that the herbs and resins are protected from the direct heat. A feather can be used to fan the charcoal embers and direct the smoke where you wish.

The smudging ritual can now begin. Once it is finished, allow the charcoal to burn out and remove the ashes and carbonized remnants of the incense materials with tongs or a spoon, or sieve the ash through a tea strainer. Don't put out the charcoal by pouring water into the bowl, as it can cause ceramic containers to crack. But if in a hurry, use the tongs to dunk the charcoal briefly in water in order to put it out.

Questions and Answers

Question: What should I do in a room fitted with a smoke detector?

Answer: Burning incense on a mesh or an essential oil diffuser generates little or no smoke and likewise incense sticks rarely produce too much smoke. When smudging on charcoal, the amount of smoke generated can be reduced by sprinkling a pinch of sand on the hot charcoal—the layer of sand provides insulation from the greatest heat. Using smaller quantities of herbs and resins also generates less smoke. Woods and resins can be chopped finely or ground using a mortar and pestle. The scents given off when there is less smoke are usually softer and less acrid, as the incense ingredients do not burn but smolder slowly.

Question: What can I do if there is too much smoke?

Answer: Try reducing the amount of herbs and resins that you are using. Make the pieces smaller and scatter a layer of sand on the charcoal. Some herbs tend to generate powerful, pungent smoke when burned on charcoal and should therefore be burned on a metal mesh instead. If there is already too much smoke in the room, try spraying a little water onto the smoke or use a room spray to help bind the particles together.

Question: Can smudging be harmful? Is it okay to breathe in the smoke?

Answer: Smudging on charcoal naturally produces smoke, but this should not be inhaled regularly over long periods of time. It is the dose, the amount of exposure to the smoke, that is relevant here. Occasional or even regular exposure to smoke from smudging should generally not be harmful for a healthy person. If you do notice you are having difficulty breathing in reaction to smudging, open all windows and leave the room. You may also wish to use a room spray or humidifier to bind the smoke particles. Try smudging using an incense burner or an essential oil heat diffuser instead. It is also important to buy high-quality herbs and resins and to be aware that some—even quite common—substances are toxic and can be burned only in small quantities (tonka and thuja, for example). Ready-made incense mixtures may contain certain amounts

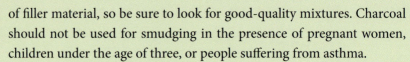

of filler material, so be sure to look for good-quality mixtures. Charcoal should not be used for smudging in the presence of pregnant women, children under the age of three, or people suffering from asthma.

Question: Can I simply blow the smoke in a certain direction rather than guiding it with a feather?

Answer: You can, of course, move smoke in any direction you wish using just your hand or breath, but in many shamanistic traditions it is a feather, as part of a wing, that incorporates the energy of the air into the ritual, uniting fire and air. Using your breath brings your own, human energy into the ritual, which is not considered desirable. It really depends on how you wish to celebrate a ritual, or whether you just want to drive away flies and mosquitoes.

Sourcing Smudging Materials

In Western countries the idea of burning incense was mainly associated with Eastern religions or perhaps, by extension, with dining in Chinese and Asian restaurants. Smudging has since become so popular that appropriate herbs, resins, and pre-mixed materials are now found in stores catering to spiritual interests and even in the practical sections of some bookshops. There is generally a good range of materials available for beginners, while those who are more experienced in search of the widest selection of top-quality herbs and resins can find what they need online. Information on the precise base plant should normally be given, but always look out for good-quality and ethical sources. The cheaper the price, the greater the chances that the incense is packed with filler or contains some form of contaminants.

Many herbs and resins do not need to be bought but can be sourced from the garden or while out walking. If you're not a wild herb expert quite yet, just remember the following rule: always consult three separate sources to identify a plant definitively. Remember that some plants are protected or endangered species, and plants should not normally be picked from nature reserves or other protected areas—if in doubt, check the regulations for your state or area. If there's any chance of confusing a poisonous or protected plant (for example, mistaking poisonous hemlock for angelica), it is wisest to leave the plant alone. In addition, plants that grow at the verges of conventional agricultural fields, busy roads, railroad lines, or where dogs may do their business are generally contaminated with toxins or bacteria.

The glossary (p. 101) contains a list of common plants that are easy to find and can be picked without a problem. Only pick as much as you need, however, so that the plant can grow back or propagate itself; a good rule of thumb is to take no more than a third of a plant at any particular location.

After picking, herbs should be dried carefully and as quickly as possible. To do so, store them somewhere warm, dry, and dark that is also well ventilated. Whole leaves and flowers should be placed on a drying frame or stored in small amounts in a paper bag; plant stalks and shoots should be hung upside down in loose bundles. Some flowers (such as mullein or rose blossom) and all roots and fruit should be dried in an oven at 100–120°F (40–50°C) so that they do not develop mold or lose too many of their active ingredients. Do not smudge with any materials that are not yet fully dry. Once dried, keep herbs and resins in a dry, dark place, ideally in an airtight glass jar or metal tin with a lid that can be closed.

Herbs dried for smudging should keep for around a year, but it's easy to tell if herbs still contain enough active ingredients. Crush or crumble a small amount between your fingers and smell them. If they give off a scent, they still contain enough active ingredients for effective smudging.

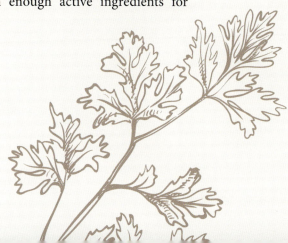

Questions and Answers

Question: Can I burn culinary herbs or do I have to buy special herbs for smudging?
Answer: It doesn't matter whether herbs (ideally organic) are obtained from the supermarket or are grown in the garden and dried at home, both sources can be used.

Question: Can I collect resins myself?
Answer: Yes, it is possible to collect resins from spruce, Scots pine, fir, and larch trees, but remember that the presence of liquid resin always indicates that a tree has been injured or that it is fighting off pests at a particular location on the trunk. Therefore, only take drops of resin that have dried and can easily be removed by hand, and note that attempting to pry off resin with an implement can cause the tree further damage.

Question: Is it acceptable to buy material taken from plants that are now rare or protected?
Answer: Always make sure that the raw materials have been ethically sourced or sustainably grown—in most cases, this is readily indicated by the price. Rare and protected herbs and resins such as white sandalwood, olibanum (frankincense) and a number of other resins found in countries of the East should be used sparingly, but common plants can in any case be substituted for most exotic herbs and resins; for example, mugwort or garden sage can be substituted for more exotic kinds of sage, and spruce resin can be used instead of frankincense.

Making blends

Give your imagination free rein and make your own smudge sticks. Why not make a blend of your favorite fragrances, or simply use whatever you have to hand in the garden. Ideally, the range of effects will complement one another along with the scents. See The Uses of Smudging chapter (p. 23) and the lists of substances arranged by application.

Herbs used in a smudging blend can be chopped, crushed between the fingers, or ground with a mortar and pestle. For herbs to be smudged on a mesh, it makes sense to use pieces that are a little larger. Don't use more than nine ingredients in a single blend, and it's best to make up only small amounts to start with to ensure you find the blend appealing.

Top tips

- Take notes while making a blend to keep a record in case you wish to make it again.
- Blends that use dried herbs alone tend to burn rather than smolder, producing a lot of smoke and a charred smell. It may therefore be preferable to burn such blends outdoors or to mix them with resin.
- When making a blend, as a guide, allow 1 part resin for every 3 to 4 parts herbs, wood, or roots. Authors Marlis Bader and Adolfine Nitschke both recommend 1 part root, 1 part wood, 1 to 2 parts resins, and 4 to 5 parts herbs.
- The more finely the ingredients are ground, the better the scents will combine and the more harmonious the overall effect will be. Very sticky resins are easier to grind when they have been frozen beforehand. Resin stains on utensils and fingers can be removed with rubbing alcohol.
- Mastic (p. 142) is a universal binding agent for all blends. It intensifies the scent of the individual elements and combines them into a harmonious whole.

The Uses of SMUDGING

This section explores just some of the many uses of herbs and resins in smudging. Some are traditional, others more contemporary, and there is plenty of opportunity for experimentation.

A list of suitable herbs and resins is provided for each recommended use so that blends of domestic kitchen herbs and more exotic ingredients can be created with ease. Don't forget the rule of thumb: 1 part resin to 3 or 4 parts herbs, wood, or root. I have also suggested a few tried-and-tested combinations for smudging blends.

Recommendations
- When a color is not specified (such as for sandalwood, sage, and copal), any color of this herb or resin can be used.
- Some herbs might be difficult to obtain, being protected or prohibited in certain countries. Please always check before use.
- If you have any allergies, have a respiratory illness, or are pregnant, please be sure to check first with a doctor that smudging is suitable for you. Pregnant women should always avoid galbanum, labdanum, and mugwort.

Acceptance

ACCEPTING SOMETHING means to acknowledge it and to recognize it for what it is. We can accept and tolerate the opinions of others without necessarily sharing or even approving of them. When we are able to accept something without taking it too personally or relating it to ourselves, we are acting with tolerance and equanimity. However, it is not just a question of accepting things, other people, and their opinions, it is almost more important to accept ourselves, with all our faults and failings, our appearance, our feelings, and the mistakes we make. It is about allowing ourselves to be just as we are, and to treat ourselves with kindness and consideration.

The opposite of self-acceptance runs the gamut of everything from self-criticism to self-hatred—there are few who have mastered the art of constructive self-criticism. Being at peace with our own emotions means allowing ourselves to feel but without suppressing any unpleasant feelings. In spiritual groups, feelings of rage, rejection, or pain can be seen as undesirable or even as faults. The expectation is that everything should constantly be "light and love" while "negative" emotions are considered a sign that an individual has not yet progressed far enough along their path to enlightenment. However, true mastery is achieved by those who acknowledge all their feelings and allow them to exist, accepting themselves as they are. Whether and how this is acted upon is another matter.

Herbs and resins that help us to accept
- put us in a cheerful and friendly mood;
- promote harmony;
- bring inner relaxation;
- clear the mind to the extent that we are able to distinguish objective evaluation from unsparing criticism;
- open the heart and enhance our capacity for love.

common: ash, lady's bedstraw, chamomile, daisy, elecampane, hops, iris, lavender, masterwort, quince, rose, rosemary, spruce, sweetgrass, verbena
exotic: agarwood, aniseed, copaiba, copal (golden), dammar gum, elemi, galbanum, guggul, gum arabic, myrrh, myrtle, sandalwood (white), styrax, tonka

Galbanum helps us to break down mental blockages and entrenched beliefs, as does iris.

Smudging blends
Harmony
benzoin, lavender, rose, sage (white), styrax, sweetgrass
Self-love
benzoin, dammar gum, elecampane, labdanum, myrrh, rose

For a smudging ritual designed to promote acceptance, it may help to accompany the ritual with a meditation. The Buddhist metta (loving kindness) meditation in particular can help us to feel more amiable and predisposed to acceptance.

Ancestors

⇨ Parting ⇨ Grief and End-of-Life Care ⇨ Annual Festivals

IN MANY CULTURES death and dying have been banished behind closed hospital doors and the body of the deceased is no longer washed or laid out by relatives. Not so in some countries, where death and caring for one's ancestors are a still a natural part of life. Not only do people still visit graves regularly, but an ancestor's remains might be kept in an urn at home with the family, perhaps on a dedicated altar, and in some cultures the remains of the dead are sometimes even brought out for ceremonies on certain days. In this way, a person's forebears are not only honored as those who came before them and gave them life, but are also a part of everyday life. In Western Christian culture, several days in November are designated as days of remembrance (All Saints' Day, All Souls' Day, and Veterans Day), when the dead are commemorated, while Halloween (the evening before All Saints' Day) is celebrated as an excuse for dressing up in scary costumes (and conspicuous consumption) whose real origins have been forgotten. Only those who wish to observe the old Nordic traditions and celebrate the annual festival of Samhain pay homage to the dead and their ancestors on the night of October 31 to November 1.

There are two ways of getting in touch with our ancestors. Firstly, we can remember them and honor the role they played in our lives (whether we have been conscious of this or not). A good way of doing this is to set up a small ancestral altar. It can be temporary or permanent, with photos and mementoes such as jewelry or something inherited that brings us closer to them. As a regular ritual and day of remembrance, a candle can be lit on their birthday and/or the anniversary of their death.

The second way to make contact is through necromancy, the questioning of ancestors, based on the assumption that those who have passed on beyond the veil are able to still advise us. Incense was traditionally used for this purpose. "Threshold herbs" (that soften the boundary between life and death) and those that promote the reception of visions are recommended, but some previous experience of engaging with the spirit world is essential for this type of inquiry to be successful.

> Suitable materials for making contact with ancestors include
> - smudging blends for Samhain;
> - plants that are indigenous to, and traditionally used in, an ancestor's homeland.
>
> **common:** angelica, elder, fir, fumitory, juniper, larch, mistletoe, mugwort, rosemary, Scots pine, spruce, St John's wort
> **exotic:** copal (black)

Smudging blends
Contact with ancestors
angelica, elder, frankincense, juniper, mugwort, spruce (resin)

Did you know? Mistletoe is a particularly powerful plant for engaging with ancestors, as are elder and angelica. The latter two plants have hollow stems through which it is said we can travel to the underworld to make contact with our ancestors. Elder is a "threshold tree" and the plant of the underworld goddess Hel. It is therefore an excellent guide on this journey, while angelica, associated with the Archangel Michael, is a protective and light-bringing traveling companion.

Annual Festivals

CERTAIN FESTIVALS happen at set times in the year. Four such festivals (the two solstices and two equinoxes), also known as solar festivals, are notably determined by the path of the sun across the skies, and are celebrated in more or less every culture. Four other festivals, known as moon or harvest festivals, depending on spiritual preferences, are oriented toward events in nature (and agriculture in particular), and are celebrated globally too, although in different ways, depending on the location and therefore the climatic conditions. Where we might celebrate the first snowdrops peeking out of a blanket of snow, the ancient Egyptians commemorated the annual flooding of the Nile that brought fertility. Christianity adopted many of these old festivals and reinterpreted them, but their original pagan core is often still recognizable. Easter, for example, is still determined by the full moon (and is celebrated on the first Sunday after the first full moon of spring), and Christmas, the birth of Christ, neatly coincides with the winter solstice. Celebrating the cycle of nature that is still ritually observed in annual festivals is known as natural religion. Simply observing natural events and when they occur (the first leaves on the trees in spring, the emergence of the first crocus flower, the migration of different bird species, when the days start to lengthen) is enough, and helps us—as humans, who have become so alienated from nature—to slot back into the cycles of the natural world. Here are a few suggestions for those who would like to give greater symbolism to these events or wish to associate them with Christian ideas.

Yule/Alban Arthan/midwinter/winter solstice

⇨ The Nights of Yuletide ⇨ Light-Bringers ⇨ Divination/Clairvoyance

The longest night, the time of greatest darkness, occurs with the winter solstice on December 21, and from this day onward, the days begin to get longer again. This return of the light is a theme that recurs in every culture, with the winter solstice being a day (or rather, a night) for both looking back and looking forward, for partings and new beginnings. In some traditions, it also marks the first of the nights of Yuletide, an evening in which all kinds of spirits are up to mischief and it is possible to catch a glimpse beyond the veil.

> **common:** angelica, fir, juniper, larch, masterwort, mistletoe, mugwort, Scots pine, spruce, St John's wort, sweetgrass
> **exotic:** bay leaf, frankincense, myrrh

Smudging blends
The nights of Yuletide
angelica, juniper, lavender, mugwort, myrtle, rosemary, sage (white), spruce (resin), verbena
Christmas
cinnamon, myrrh, palo santo, spruce (needles), tonka

Imbolc

⇨ New Beginnings and Transition ⇨ Cleansing

The first signs of life in nature are celebrated at Imbolc (February 1), also known as St Brigid's Day, one of Ireland's patron saints. Snowdrops and birch trees are traditionally closely associated with this time, one of new beginnings. In the past it was also a day on which the devout would pray for blessings, since the coldest time of the year, when winter supplies would run low, was often still to come. It is a time to think about what ideas and passions are to be awakened in the coming year, what seeds are to be sown. Imbolc was also a day on which a cleansing smudging ritual would traditionally be carried out in the home and in the stalls and barns sheltering animals.

> **common:** birch, elecampane, marigold, St John's wort
> **exotic:** mastic

Smudging blends

Imbolc
birch, elecampane, mastic, mugwort, rosemary

Ostara/Alban Eilir/spring equinox

⇨ Cleansing

Ostara is celebrated on March 20, the spring equinox, a day of balance before the light and sun-filled but also busy time of summer begins. The last snows have now melted and what began to stir at Imbolc is now starting to grow. This day represents another opportunity to think about what should be sown this year.

> **common:** birch, elecampane, lavender
> **exotic:** cardamom, copal, nutmeg, myrrh

Beltane/Walpurgis

⇨ Energy and Vitality ⇨ Love and Sensuality

Beltane, which is celebrated on May 1 or during the night of April 30 to May 1 (or also on the second full moon of spring) is a festival of pure vitality, love, passion, and joy in life, and is a time of growth and change. Many customs, such as dancing around a maypole or May tree (hawthorn), have been preserved and are still practiced to this day across the world. Nature is now in full bloom, and even people find they have a spring in their step.

> **common:** lady's mantle, mugwort, rose, rosemary
> **exotic:** benzoin, cinnamon, myrtle, styrax

Smudging blends
Beltane
cardamom, elder, rose, sandalwood (red)

Litha/Alban Hefin/midsummer/ summer solstice

⇨ Light-Bringers

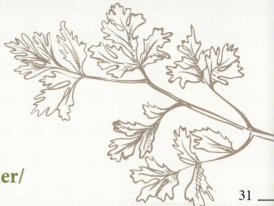

The summer solstice on June 21 marks the height of summer, the high point of the power of light and the sun. It is around this time that sunflowers and various light-bringing plants are in bloom (and have the greatest powers of healing). Celebrations for the solstice are carried out all over the world with festivals and gatherings. Bonfires are traditionally lit in some countries, prompting reflection on what habits, thoughts, or attitudes should be consigned to the flames. St John's wort and mugwort are an essential part of this festival.

> **common:** angelica, chamomile, elder, elecampane, mistletoe, mugwort, rose, St John's wort, sweetgrass, thyme, verbena
> **exotic:** copal, myrrh, frankincense

Lughnasadh/Lammas

Lughnasadh is the first of the three harvest festivals and is celebrated on August 1. It marks the beginning of the harvest and is a festival of thanksgiving and hope but also of farewell. On this day we think of the seeds that we too have sown and the harvest we have reaped. It is a good day to pick herbs whose healing powers are particularly strong at this time, for example, as traditional herb bundles.

> **common:** lady's bedstraw, chamomile, elecampane, meadowsweet, mint, mugwort, mullein, solidago, St John's wort, thyme, yarrow
> **exotic:** frankincense, myrrh

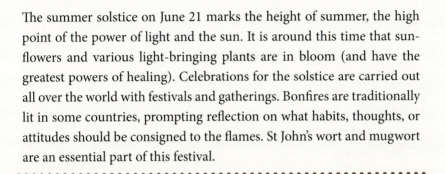

Mabon/Alban Elfed/autumn equinox

⇨ Blessing and Consecration

Mabon is the second of the three harvest festivals and is celebrated on September 21 to coincide with the autumn equinox, like the Christian harvest festival. It is a day of balance, signalling the beginning of the dark season of the year, and with it a time of peace and reflection. The theme is abundance, the year's harvest, and how this is to be shared and appreciated. This includes not only material abundance, but also our talents and experiences. It is also the day on which we should thank nature (and God, or the gods), perhaps by carrying out a smudging ritual.

> **common:** angelica, elecampane, lavender, rose, rosemary, St John's wort, sweetgrass
> **exotic:** aniseed, benzoin, cinnamon, frankincense, myrrh

Smudging blends
Mabon
copaiba, coriander, juniper, sweetgrass, yerba santa

Samhain

⇨ Ancestors ⇨ Letting Go ⇨ Divination and Clairvoyance ⇨ Dreams

Samhain, the third of the harvest festivals, which Western culture has adopted as Halloween and turned into a fancy-dress party, particularly for children, is traditionally celebrated on the evening of October 31, the night before All Saints' Day. In Celtic culture, Samhain is the festival that marks the end of harvest and rings in the New Year, which starts with days of darkness. It is a time to remember our ancestors and all those who have died, a tradition that has been kept alive by Christianity. As the veil to the next world is particularly thin during this period, it is a very favorable time for divination, dream work, and smudging for protection and cleansing.

> **common:** angelica, elder, fir, fumitory, juniper, larch, mistletoe, mugwort, pine, spruce, St John's wort
> **exotic:** copal (black), frankincense

Smudging blends
Contacting ancestors
angelica, elder, frankincense, juniper, mugwort, spruce (resin)

Blessing and Consecration

⇨ New Beginnings and Transition

TO BLESS SOMETHING means not only to wish an undertaking, a person, or a situation well, but also to affirm and strengthen the good in it. It is a manifestation of a successful outcome or achieved goal, or simply of happiness and contentment. In a religious context, a blessing is a request for divine protection and help, often in a set formula such as a prayer.

Smudging that brings blessings brings light energies into a cleansed space or person so that life can continue in the best possible way, without interference from low-vibrating energies.

Consecration or dedication involves devoting something to a sacred purpose, sanctifying it in a sense. This process turns an everyday object into a ritual item, a normal person into a priest or priestess. The act of consecration reinforces the idea of being destined for a special purpose, with incense being used to accompany a ceremony of consecration in almost all cultures.

Both blessing and consecration therefore mean charging something or someone with good energy. Some of the herbs and resins used in blessings also have cleansing properties (such as angelica, mugwort, and thyme), while when using others, it makes sense to first perform a separate smudging ritual for cleansing. This is especially true if ritual items are to be consecrated.

> Herbs and resins that consecrate and bring blessings
> - charge with energy;
> - attract good energies (benevolent spirits);
> - open the heart and promote gratitude;
> - are dedicated to particular divinities (sweetgrass and mugwort are both associated with Mary, the mother of Jesus, and the Norse goddess Freya; mugwort is also linked with Freya, Isis, Artemis, and Diana).
>
> **common:** angelica, lady's bedstraw, chamomile, elder, elecampane, fumitory, hyssop, lavender, meadowsweet, mistletoe, mugwort, oak, rose, rosemary, St John's wort, sweetgrass, thyme, verbena
> **exotic:** bay leaf, calamus, cinnamon, copal (white), cypress, dragon's blood, frankincense, guggul, myrrh, opoponax, sage (white), sandalwood, tonka

Frankincense is, of course, the best-known herb or resin for blessing and consecration.

Smudging blends

Blessing the home I
cinnamon, dammar gum, elecampane, iris, lavender, myrrh, orange, patchouli

Blessing the home II
benzoin, frankincense, juniper, mugwort, myrrh, sweetgrass

Ritual

A ritual for blessing a house or the home can be performed in the same way as a cleansing ritual and is described in Nights of Yuletide (p. 82).

A small blessing ritual

To bless yourself, an undertaking, or an object, prepare in the usual way by centering yourself, and carefully and mindfully assembling the smudging equipment. Choose some suitable herbs and resins.

Place the object or something that represents what you wish to bless in front of you. Light the charcoal and once it has reached the correct heat, place the first portion of herbs and resins on top. Take the object to be blessed or consecrated (or the representative token) and hold it in the smoke from the incense. Imagine the smoke removing all the negative energies, all the chaos, and everything unwanted that are clinging to this object, and carrying them away into the sky. At the same time, picture the object filling with light and blessings. You might like to set an intention at this point; for example, "May this undertaking be blessed," "May this object be blessed for this purpose," or "May I be blessed." Continue the smudging ritual until everything feels light, relaxed, and right, and bring the ritual to an end in your own way.

Clarity

⇨ Concentration ⇨ Cleansing

BY DEFINITION, on the one hand clarity describes the condition of transparency, with nothing to pollute or cloud things, and on the other, the clear comprehension of an issue. If a mountain stream is clear, we can see right to the bottom. If instructions are presented to us with clarity, there are no misunderstandings. If our minds are clear, with no half-conscious thoughts and emotions in the background, we find it easy to make decisions and concentrate on our goals. In a state of clarity, we can weigh up advantages and disadvantages, identify obstacles, and formulate strategies. When we consider that our thoughts as well as our words shape our life circumstances, it becomes obvious that a desired outcome cannot be achieved with chaotic or confused thoughts.

> Herbs and resins can help us to achieve clarity and/or to order our thoughts by
> - freeing us and our surroundings of external energies;
> - enhancing our powers of concentration;
> - benefiting from their calming and relaxing properties;
> - refreshing us and putting new wind in our sails.
>
> **common:** birch, elecampane, hyssop, juniper, larch, mint, rosemary, sage, solidago, spruce, verbena
> **exotic:** bay leaf, camphor, cedar, cedar (American), copal (white and golden), cypress, dammar gum, eucalyptus, frankincense, galangal, mastic, myrrh, myrtle, vetiver

Smudging blends
Fresh impetus
birch, calamus, frankincense, galangal, mint
Attentiveness
camphor, copal (white), frankincense, myrtle, rosemary, verbena

Ritual

Bringing clarity into our lives can begin with the simple tidying of our surroundings (external disorder reflects inner disorder and vice versa) and perhaps by performing a cleansing smudging session (p. 38) that will drive away external energies and energy vampires. After all, what else are external energies but contaminants that rob us of clear sight? If, after this, your mind still feels disordered and confused, try the following ritual.

Clear sight

Take a moment to collect your thoughts and center yourself in the present. Prepare your smudging equipment and choose a smudging blend. Do not worry too much about the choice of incense materials. The more clarity you gain during smudging, the more confident your intuition will be when selecting incense materials in general. Light the charcoal and when it has reached the correct heat, place the first portion of incense on top. Breathe in the scent, and initially just feel it entering your body and penetrating your senses. Now imagine your mind or your emotions as a lake. Observe how the lake looks. Is the water clear? How deep is it, can you see to the bottom? Is the wind blowing waves across it or is the surface of the water calm? Just observe for a moment, without judging. You might notice other details—the shore might be sandy or there might be vegetation growing right down to the waterline. Perhaps ducks are swimming across it, or you can see water lilies or even trash. When you have fully observed the lake, breathe in deeply, and take the decision to calm and clear the water. You might like to set an intention, saying aloud or silently to yourself for example, "My mind is now becoming calm and clear." Now imagine the scent of the incense wafting over the lake as the ducks slowly swim to shore, the trash sinks beneath the surface, the wind drops, the waves subside, and the water becomes clear. Breathe in this calm atmosphere and hold the image of a deep, clear, clean lake in your mind for as long as feels right. When you are ready, thank the lake, and finish the ritual. Relax and enjoy the sense of inner peace.

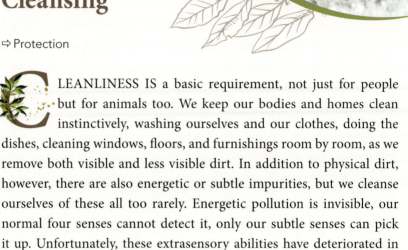

Cleansing

⇨ Protection

CLEANLINESS IS a basic requirement, not just for people but for animals too. We keep our bodies and homes clean instinctively, washing ourselves and our clothes, doing the dishes, cleaning windows, floors, and furnishings room by room, as we remove both visible and less visible dirt. In addition to physical dirt, however, there are also energetic or subtle impurities, but we cleanse ourselves of these all too rarely. Energetic pollution is invisible, our normal four senses cannot detect it, only our subtle senses can pick it up. Unfortunately, these extrasensory abilities have deteriorated in most people, so our knowledge, or rather our instinct, that we should cleanse ourselves on the subtle plane as well, has also been forgotten. Nonetheless, we acquire subtle impurities—external energies—just as easily as we pick up physical dirt.

These external energies include
- energies from our own thoughts and feelings;
- energies from the thoughts and feelings of others;
- energies from the previous inhabitants (both living and dead) of our home;
- earth-bound souls, nature spirits, and other subtle entities ("ghosts");
- radiation rom the Earth, water veins, and electrosmog.

The energies we experience as "pollution" are those with low vibrations and are destructive or unpleasant. Conflict, anger, fear, addiction, envy, deprivation, and so on, generate frequencies that weigh us down, while we experience places and people in which contentment, love, and happiness predominate as pleasant and comforting. External energies may be present in a room or become attached to us—people might say that the atmosphere is bad or that something is sucking the air from a room. Sensitive people are aware of, and can tell the difference between, these energies very clearly.

When folk magic speaks of evil spirits, demons, and charms, they can be understood as symbolic representations of negative energies. Thoughts, words, and deeds generate energy, and if they are spoken or carried out with ill will, the effect is like an evil spell. Even if no curses are actively directed against us, it is possible subconsciously to pick up on another's bad mood hanging over them like a black cloud.

It is much the same with defense against disease. Although ancient Greek physician Hippocrates described substances in the air that caused sickness (miasmas or impurities), a clear connection between microorganisms and infectious diseases was not established until 1876, by German physician Robert Koch. Prior to this, popular belief blamed witches for inflicting disease or demons for causing sickness in livestock. Pathogens (protozoa, bacteria, viruses, and fungal spores) lie somewhere between energetic and physical contamination, materially present but imperceptible to the senses. It is no surprise to learn that those medicinal plants that were used against the evil eye or to protect against demons have since been shown to have antibacterial, disinfectant, or antiseptic properties. Smudging used for cleansing purposes is therefore intended to clear the atmosphere in a room, an object, or a person's aura of tension, low vibration energies, evil spirits, and pathogens.

> Cleansing herbs and resins
> - promote positive energies and so raise vibration overall;
> - reduce tension;
> - ward off demons, witches, and the evil eye;
> - cultivate a person's aura;
> - have antiseptic properties.
>
> **common:** amber, angelica root, bedstraw, fumitory, hyssop, juniper, meadowsweet, mistletoe, mugwort, oak, rosemary, sage, solidago, spruce, thyme
> **exotic:** asafetida, bay leaf, camphor, cedar, cedar (American), cloves, copal (white), dragon's blood, elemi, galbanum, palo santo, sage (white), sandalwood, sweetgrass

Smudging blends

Classic cleansing
angelica, cedar, copal, sage (white), sweetgrass

Deep cleansing
camphor, frankincense, fumitory, mugwort

Blessings and well-being
cinnamon dammar gum, elecampane, lavender, myrrh, orange, orris root, patchouli

New home
elecampane, juniper, lavender, sweetgrass

Rituals

Energetic house cleansing

Before attempting to cleanse the home energetically with a smudging ritual, it is important to clean it physically. Dust, clutter, and junk cause energy to stagnate, and external energies can build up wherever the flow of energy starts to falter. The cleaner the home is physically, the less disruptive energy can accumulate inside it.

Once your apartment or house has been thoroughly cleaned and tidied, a smudging session can be carried out. It is important to begin by opening the windows. Just as hospital wards should be well ventilated so that bacteria-laden air can escape, at least one window should be open during (or at the very least after) cleansing the home so that any disruptive or harmful energies can leave the space.

Begin by grounding and centering yourself in a way that is best for you. The more stable and balanced you feel, the more successful the cleansing ritual will be. Therefore, if you are feeling stressed, emotional, or on edge, it would be better to begin with self-cleansing. Set your intention, saying it out aloud or silently to yourself (for example, "I wish to cleanse my home of all disruptive influences"). Now prepare your smudging equipment, paying close attention to the ingredients you choose—perhaps a ready-made blend that you have used before, or use your intuition to make the selection. Since herbs normally burn quickly and produce a lot of smoke, the ideal blend for this ritual would be resin based, or cover the charcoal with a layer of sand to reduce the heat.

Once the incense starts to smolder, the ritual can begin. Take the smudging bowl and carry it through all the rooms in your home. There is no set rule to the sequence in which you should take the rooms, but if more than one story is involved, working your way up from the bottom to the top has proven effective. However, it is a good idea to work out a route in advance in order not to miss out an area by mistake. Enter each room and fan the smoke around so that it penetrates into every corner. Trust your instinct. You may feel that the energy in some parts of the room is denser and darker than in others, or perhaps there is a change in the way the smoke rises. Continue the session for as long as feels right for you. You might like to repeat your intention silently, like a mantra or prayer.

Be sure to open one or more windows (if you have not already done so) so that all the old energy can escape together with the smoke. Once you have been through every room, consciously thank the plants and resins that have made themselves available to you and, if you wish to do so, use an energy or spray of water to bind the smoke particles floating in the air. You can now let the charcoal burn down.

You might also like to make use the residual heat of the charcoal to add more incense. The degree to which a room's energy is drained depends on the ingredients used. Some herbs and resins act equally upon both good and bad energies and cleanse both. To ensure that what may now be an energy vacuum is not filled with undesirable energies, it makes sense to carry out a smudging that promotes blessings, or simply one that makes you feel happy and cheerful. If you are planning, for example, a spiritual ritual in your home or know that you have an unconscious tendency to invite in "spirits," burn a blend of protective incense to keep the good energies in the room.

Bring the ritual to a close by sensing this renewed feeling of space and perhaps relaxing with a cup of tea.

Energetic self-cleansing

Begin the ritual by grounding and centering yourself in the way that is best for you. You might like to set an intention, for example, saying aloud or silently to yourself, "I wish to free my body from disruptive influences on every level." Prepare your smudging utensils, paying close attention to the blend of ingredients that you choose—either a ready-made blend or using your intuition to make the selection.

Once the charcoal is smoldering, the session can begin. There are no set rules for a self-cleansing ritual, but it generally takes the form of one of the following two procedures.

Option 1: Place the bowl with the smoldering herbs and spices on the floor and stand over it, allowing the smoke to drift up over your body, bathing you in its power. Visualize it carrying away all disruptive energies and cleansing you internally as well as externally.

Option 2: Take the smudging bowl in your hands and hold it level with your heart, breathing in the scent of the burning herbs. Now fan the smoke and bathe each part of your body with it in turn, from the soles of your feet, along your arms, to the top of your head. If you are performing this ritual together with another person, bathe each other in the smoke. Work with each part of the body for as long as feels right and good. As with cleansing living space, some parts of the body may feel heavier, denser, or darker than others. Visualize the smoke carrying away all the disruptive energies that you have acquired and cleansing you within as well.

Focus on your body, think about how every part is now feeling, and take a moment to thank the plants and resins that have given their essence for you. Allow the charcoal to burn down. As with cleansing the home, it can make sense to protect and energize the body after a self-cleansing ritual by burning more incense. You might therefore like to make use of what remains of the hot charcoal and add more incense to it. Bring the ritual to a close in a relaxing way, such as by listening to some music or drinking a cup of tea.

Questions and Answers

Question: Do I have to follow a particular route or direction when cleansing the house?

Answer: There are as many suggestions as there are traditions in this respect. Some practitioners recommend cleansing a house from bottom to top (from the basement to the upper floors), but others the precise opposite. Some recommend working clockwise, others prefer to work anticlockwise, others again suggest working in a star shape. As a beginner, it makes sense to pay attention to your own gut feeling and intuition when making your choice.

Question: And what about self-cleansing?

Answer: Again, there is no one correct way, a self-cleansing ritual may begin at the level of the heart, for example, as this is naturally the level at which most people would hold the smudging bowl in front of them, especially if intending to add more herbs. This is also a good moment to center yourself once more and to set an intention. You can either work with the smoke down to your feet and then up to your head, or vice versa. Rely on your intuition to sense how long the ritual should be.

Question: Should I use the same smudging blend every time?

Answer: Yes and no. Generally speaking, part of the effectiveness of the ritual is based on automatic conditioning. If we do something on a regular basis, such as habitually wear a certain item of clothing or carry out a particular act in a particular place, we begin to associate it with a specific mood or state of consciousness or mind. As scents directly affect the limbic system, the effect of incense is even greater. On the other hand, the rule in herbal medicine is that the active substances from a medicinal plant should not be used for longer than six weeks, otherwise the body can become habituated to them and their effects will begin to reduce. This is why it can make sense to vary the components of an incense blend for treating physical complaints (due to the pharmacological effects), while for ritual purposes and an energetic effect, it can be more beneficial to keep to the same blend or just one main scent ingredient.

> **Question:** Why should I not use my breath to blow the smoke to direct it?
>
> **Answer:** We rely on the essence and energy of plants, especially when used as part of a protective and cleansing smudging blend. Our breath possesses its own energy, and if used would disrupt the cleansing effect. Ultimately, we would be filling the room with our own energy through our breath.

Concentration

⇨ Clarity ⇨ Acceptance

CONCENTRATION DESCRIBES the ability to occupy ourselves with something—a question, problem, or some kind of issue—without deviating or being distracted (or distracting ourselves, which is far more common!). Our attention is fixed and focused. These days, with information routinely presented in "bite-size chunks" and TV programs being interrupted by frequent breaks, many find it hard to concentrate. It's no coincidence that students from certain Asian countries, where discipline and regular practice are important features of the education system, perform best in math competitions—the ability to solve complex mathematical problems is directly connected with being able to stay focused. The ability to concentrate involves willpower and perseverance—we have to work at paying attention. When we are tired, we find it difficult to apply ourselves, and before we can focus, we need clarity. This is why it is recommended that parents whose children are just starting school provide them with a quiet workspace that is easy to keep tidy, helping children to concentrate better and study without distractions. However, we are not always in a position to switch off the commotion of everything that is going on around us and have to focus even amid the hustle and bustle. Just look at the conditions in which people in India, for example, are still able to meditate or practice yoga.It takes a certain amount of self-discipline and mental control to ignore disruptions and to block them out. It is all too easy to do the opposite and focus on whatever is disturbing us. As whatever is causing the disruption intrudes upon our thoughts, instead of serenity and calm, we feel aggression. We can break this downward spiral with an incense ritual. As is so often the case, just the simple act of performing the ritual can be effective.

> Powers of concentration can be improved by herbs and resins that
> - are relaxing;
> - clear and focus the mind;
> - are stimulating and provide the energy required to summon up willpower;
> - stimulate and wake us up;
> - bring inner peace.
>
> **common:** birch, elecampane, hyssop, juniper, lemon balm, mint, oak, rosemary, spruce, verbena
>
> **exotic:** bay leaf, calamus, cardamom, cinnamon, cypress, elemi, eucalyptus, gum arabic, nutmeg, patchouli

Smudging blends
Attentiveness
camphor, copal (white), frankincense, myrtle, rosemary, verbena
Concentration
elecampane, copal (white), frankincense, lavender, rose, styrax, verbena

Ritual
If bringing order to your environment by decluttering, cleaning, and tidying aren't helping you to focus, try the ritual on the following page. You may also find the clear sight ritual (p. 37) useful.

Focus on your goal
Gather your thoughts, center yourself, and be in the present moment. Think about your goal and on what you wish to—or have to—concentrate. Now light the charcoal and when it has reached the correct heat, place the first portion of herbs and resins on top. Breathe in the fragrance and think about how you are feeling right now. Are you restless? Where are your thoughts wandering? Are you conscious of something small that is irritating you? Can you hear a noise somewhere? Breathe in the scent of the incense and imagine the smoke wrapping itself around all these intrusive elements (whether internal or external), rolling them up into a bundle and carrying them off into the sky. Now imagine your consciousness as the beam from a flashlight and point it at your goal. Watch your goal light up in your mind's eye as every detail becomes clear, see how it grows larger and captures your full attention. Perhaps you can already make out the solution, if there is one, or you can see important details that you had previously missed. Observe your goal caught in the beam of the flashlight for as long as you wish.

Once you feel the ritual has reached a natural conclusion, let the charcoal burn down. Before you relax completely, make a note of the insights you have achieved.

Courage and Self-Confidence

⇨ Energy and Vitality ⇨ Parting ⇨ Letting Go ⇨ New Beginnings and Transition ⇨ Fear and Anxiety

BEING BRAVE does not mean not being afraid. A courageous person acts despite their fear, remaining focused and believing in themselves and a good outcome for their aspirations. All too often we remain in situations that are not (or are no longer) good for us. A job that doesn't feel right, a marriage that has long been over, a home that is now too big for us . . . all because we fear change. However, a change leading to something new can in fact only be better, even if the uncertainty surrounding it may seem more threatening than the current situation. There may be apprehension and legitimate concerns, but if we believe in ourselves and our abilities, we can overcome all kinds of challenges, and it's even better if we can awaken the spirit of adventure within us!

> Herbs and resins that help us to summon up courage and be self-confident
> - clear and focus the mind;
> - bring vigor and energy;
> - help us to accept saying goodbye to the old and dare to make new beginnings.
>
> **common:** angelica, elecampane, juniper, larch, masterwort, mullein, rosemary, sage, Scots pine, solidago, spruce, thyme, verbena
> **exotic:** calamus, camphor, cedar, cloves, galangal, myrrh, styrax, sage (white)

Smudging blends
Self-confidence
elecampane, frankincense, mint, sage, spruce, thyme
Trust in life
dammar gum, elecampane, mullein, rose

Creativity and Inspiration

⇨ Meditation and Inner Vision ⇨ Concentration

MANY OF US have a creative pursuit as a hobby—making something with our hands, painting, knitting, rustling up a meal from whatever is left in the refrigerator …, all of which require creativity. Unfortunately, it is often the case that as soon as we have finished our chores and finally have some free time to devote to personal projects, the creative juices refuse to flow and a paralyzing, leaden weight descends, blocking our train of thought. It is even worse if we have to be creative on a professional level. There is nothing quite like doing something because we have to do it, rather than because we want to do it, to have a stultifying effect on the imagination.

Exercising creativity requires a similar attitude to play, which is ultimately what creativity is, a lightness of spirit. For ideas to flow, we have to be open and receptive, but equally for those ideas to bear fruit, we need concentration and focus in order not to be distracted by our surroundings or our own thoughts.

Besides facilitating the flow of ideas, successful creative work also requires inspiration—an idea that explodes into life and gets a project up and running, a brilliant idea that sometimes even we are unsure as to where it has come from. It might make us wonder if, as the literal meaning of "inspiration" might suggest, an idea really was breathed into us from some higher plane. Even to simply spot the spark of an idea, and certainly before we can fan it into a flame, we have to open ourselves up to the subtle spheres and be receptive. This is where performing a smudging ritual can help. We interrupt our daily routine, we might even escape our usual surroundings and burn incense outdoors or at a special location that we don't associate with work or chores. By being mindful of each step of the ritual, we can concentrate and relax at the same time.

When choosing incense ingredients, focus on what you need right now and select herbs and resins that
- calm and clear the mind;
- give your thoughts free rein;
- stimulate the senses;
- promote focus and concentration;
- open the mind to ideas and inspiration.

common: birch, hops, mint, rosemary, spruce, yarrow
exotic: bay leaf, benzoin, calamus, cinnamon flower buds, copal, frankincense, labdanum, myrrh, patchouli, star anis, tonka

Smudging blends
Creative flow
birch, iris, lady's mantle, myrrh, tonka, yarrow

Divination and Clairvoyance

⇨ Dreams ⇨ Stress and Tension ⇨ The Nights of Yuletide
⇨ Meditation and Inner Vision ⇨ Clarity

VIRTUALLY EVERY CULTURE has at one time had a tradition of using psychoactive plants in rituals—perhaps extracted in a drink, as an ointment, or burned in smudging—to provide a glimpse into the spirit world and the future. Will the harvest be a good one? Will the coming winter be harsh? When is the best time to sow seeds? Will a neighboring village attack? All questions of vital importance for the survival of the community. Divination and clairvoyance can take place when in a state of consciousness, but are more common in a deep or even light trance, or in dreams.

Lists of plant combinations intended to encourage visions have been found on Egyptian papyri. They include mandrake, henbane, blue lotus, poppy, wild rue, and thorn apple (*Datura stramonium*), and were burned in honor of the oracle god Ammon. Incense such as laurel, frankincense, myrrh, and labdanum were burned to promote prophetic dreams by Pythia, priestess of the well-known sacred Oracle of Delphi in ancient Greece. On the face of it, this combination sounds relatively harmless, but we can probably assume that poisonous plants such as henbane and/or datura were also involved. Ritual smudging using verbena and mistletoe is recorded among the Germanic and Celtic peoples, although the use of hemp flowers, yew, henbane, datura, and various poisonous mushrooms was also common. Just as with South American psychoactive drink ayahuasca, the use of all these psychedelic and hallucinogenic substances was strictly reserved for the priests, witch doctors, and shamans, and they were integrated into rituals and ceremonies. Many of these plants were considered sacred and making use of them in another context was regarded as sacrilege. Fortunately, there are enough mildly effective herbs and resins available in the modern age for the average person to be able to open their mind and senses without resorting to poisonous substances.

Certain moments during the course of the year—and indeed in life—are particularly suitable for clairvoyance and divination. They include the nights of Yuletide (notably Christmas Eve and New Year), when it is traditional to look to the future to see what it may hold, which is why Yuletide smudging blends are generally helpful for receiving visions of what is to come. Other days/nights when the future may be divined include Samhain and Beltane, when the veil between this world and the next is said to be thin and it is easier to glimpse "the other side."

In terms of the cycle of human lives, it is the transitional phases, the times when we are on the threshold of change, that are ideal for looking to the future, such as the progression from child to adult and then on to the wisdom of older age, but also times of great upheaval such as moving house or changing job.

It is preferable not to see divination and clairvoyance as something to practice for fun but as a conscious ritual. The incense not only promotes divination and clirvoyance through its consciousness-expanding active ingredients, but also by helping to put us in the appropriate state of mind.

> Herbs and resins conducive to divination and clairvoyance include those that
> - open the mind;
> - encourage dreams or prophetic visions and help us to remember dreams;
> - ease access to the subconscious;
> - connect with the spirit world;
> - promote a meditative state.
>
> **common:** angelica, ash, elder, elecampane, hops, juniper, mistletoe, mugwort, mullein, verbena, yarrow
> **exotic:** bay leaf, copal (white), elemi, labdanum, mastic, myrrh, myrtle, nutmeg

Smudging blends
Lucid dreams
bay leaf, hops, myrrh, myrtle, verbena
A glimpse beyond the veil
frankincense, juniper, mistletoe, mugwort, spruce (resin), verbena

Dreams

⇨ Evening Smudging Session ⇨ Divination and Clairvoyance

DREAMS ARE SAID to be whispers from the soul. We process the events of the day in our dreams, working through and cataloging our memories, learning and processing what drives us. In effect, we cleanse ourselves in our dreams. The more unfinished the trains of thought that we take to bed, the more confused our dreams since they reflect our mental energy. This is why a relaxing, cleansing smudging session in the evening, designed to clear the mind, is the perfect choice.

Dreams have other functions, however. In dreams we can obtain answers to the questions that come from deep within our subconscious, from the deepest layers of the soul. We can receive visions, signs, and messages that come from higher spheres. We may even have prophetic or lucid dreams, or follow a path of initiation within a dream.

For all these forms of dreaming, it is necessary to first clear and "tidy" the subconscious so that the mind has the space in which to open up to any images and messages that may arise (or descend).

> Herbs and resins suitable for dealing with dreams
> - make us receptive;
> - open us up to higher spheres;
> - allow us to access the deepest layers of the soul;
> - help us remember our dreams when we awaken.
>
> **common:** hops, lavender, lemon balm, mistletoe, mugwort, valerian, verbena
> **exotic:** bay leaf, copal, mastic

Smudging blends

Dreams I
dammar gum, juniper, mastic, mistletoe, mugwort, verbena

Dreams II
bay leaf, frankincense, hops, verbena, yarrow

Ritual

The ritual described in Evening Smudging Sessions (p. 55) can be used to influence our dreams.

Energy and Vitality

⇨ Grounding ⇨ Concentration

JUST AS SOME smudging blends are designed to calm and relax, others energize, revitalize, and stimulate. When feeling disheartened, unsure, and in need of encouragement, or perhaps just physically exhausted and in need of energy, instead of drinking a cup of coffee, enjoy a herbal infusion or perform a smudging session with rosemary or resins from domestic coniferous trees for a warming, energizing effect.

> Herbs and resins that revitalize and fortify
> - improve the circulation;
> - provide grounding, clearing and centering the mind;
> - refresh;
> - stimulate and wake up;
> - provide a warming effect.
>
> **common:** angelica, elecampane, fir, hyssop, juniper, mint, mugwort, oak, rosemary, sage, Scots pine, spruce, thyme, verbena
> **exotic:** calamus, camphor, cardamom, cedar, cinnamon, cloves, copal (white), cypress, dragon's blood, elemi, eucalyptus, galangal, mastic, myrrh, nutmeg, sage (white)

Rosemary and juniper are both stimulants (so those with high blood pressure or suffering from epilepsy must be careful), whereas cinnamon and cloves warm, inspire, and stimulate, and verbena helps with the making of decisions and activates inner strength. Aniseed, lemon verbena, mint, and white copal are all refreshing.

Highly energizing and stimulating herbs and resins should not be burned just before going to bed; instead use warming and relaxing plants. Including a dash of the color red (such as from dragon's blood or red sandalwood) enhances the effects of energizing blends.

Smudging blends
Strength and clarity I
angelica, dragon's blood, juniper, mugwort, olibanum, sandalwood (white)
Strength and clarity II
amber, cedar, juniper, mugwort, sage (white)
Self-confidence
bay leaf, cedar, guaiac, mugwort, myrrh, oak, spruce (resin)
Warmth and energy
cedar, cinnamon, cloves, galangal, myrrh, sandalwood (red)

Evening Smudging Sessions

⇨ Dreams ⇨ Stress and Tension

WE ARE ALL familiar with the scenario of cramming as much as possible into an evening, perhaps doing long-neglected chores, watching TV, catching up on the news, or getting annoyed by comments we read on social media. As soon as we finally hit the sheets, we lie awake forever as our mind races and we worry away at problems, which are often played out in crazy dreams when we finally do get to sleep.

A smudging session at the end of the day can help on a number of levels. The ritual of smudging itself—preparing the space, setting out the utensils, choosing or blending the herbs and resins, waiting for the charcoal to reach the right temperature—all contribute to the moment, and the ritual is also a way of bringing closure to the events of the day. It helps the mind to find rest and wind down for the evening. Depending on the plants that have been selected, the scent of the incense can gently steer you in the right direction.

Herbs and resins suitable for evening smudging sessions
- clear both atmosphere and aura, freeing us from any of the day's energies that may still be clinging to us (including the impressions of our feelings), helping us to see things clearly;
- calm the mind;
- relax the body's muscles and prepare it for sleep;
- encourage pleasant dreams and help us to remember them (if we wish to do so);
- help us to feel at one with ourselves.

common: elecampane, hops, lavender, verbena
exotic: agarwood, asafetida, benzoin, cedar, cinnamon, copal (golden), galbanum, myrrh, sandalwood, spikenard, styrax

Smudging blends

Mental and physical peace

agarwood, asafetida, cinnamon, galbanum, hops, lavender, sandalwood, spikenard, verbena

Calming anxiety, reducing stress

benzoin, cinnamon, cedar, copal (golden), elecampane, frankincense, galbanum, myrrh, sandalwood, styrax

Relaxation

benzoin, copal, lavender, rose blossom, sandalwood (white), styrax

Regeneration

cedar (wood), frankincense, lavender, sandalwood

Egyptian *kyphi* (a compound incense) is a classic choice for an evening session. It can be bought ready-made or look for a recipe online.

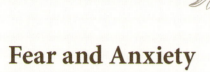

Fear and Anxiety

⇨ Stress and Tension ⇨ Letting Go ⇨ Grounding

FEAR SERVES AN important function: the stress hormones that are released prompt the fight-or-flight response, whose purpose it is to extricate us from dangerous situations as quickly as possible. Evolution has yet to catch up with the changes in our lifestyle, however. We are less likely to be attacked by predators these days, and even other moments of genuine alarm (such as narrowly escaping being involved in a road accident) tend to be rare. Today, fear is more likely to result from worries about the future or to be triggered by a physiological reaction to the relentlessly high levels of stress that we experience. Our expectations (and others' expectations of us) cause inner tension that in some people can be expressed as aggression, in others as feelings of fear ranging from apprehension and nervousness to anxiety disorders and even panic attacks. Caught between the trauma of the past and misgivings about the future, we are sometimes barely even conscious of the present in which we actually physically live.

Herbs and resins that help to combat fear and anxiety
- are calming;
- relax the body and the muscles;
- bolster the nerves;
- center the mind on the present, ensuring mental clarity;
- ground and lead us out of the mind and into the body.

common: lady's bedstraw, chamomile, elecampane, hops, larch, lavender, lemon balm, mint, rose, Scots pine, spruce, sweetgrass, verbena, yarrow
exotic: agarwood, benzoin, calamus, cardamom, cedar (American), cinnamon, copaiba, copal (golden), galbanum, myrrh, myrtle, opoponax, patchouli, sandalwood, spikenard, styrax, tonka, vetiver

Smudging blends
Balance and relaxation
benzoin, copal, lavender, rose blossom, sandalwood (white), styrax
Relaxation with common herbs and resins
resin from trees such as larch or spruce, St John's wort, verbena, yarrow
Inner peace
benzoin Sumatra, cinnamon, lavender, orange peel, rose, styrax, tonka
Achieving inner tranquility
frankincense, iris, lavender, palo santo, patchouli, tonka

Ritual
When feeling anxious or sensing an impending panic attack, the most important thing is to change your mindset. The simple act of burning incense in a smudging ritual—transitioning from thought to action—can be helpful in itself. Performing each step of the ritual consciously and in a mindful way interrupts racing thoughts that trap us in the past or worry about the future, bringing us back to the present moment.

Activating the senses
Be sure to allow yourself enough time to carry out the ritual; it is important not to feel rushed. Take a few deep breaths and prepare your chosen space. Be mindful and give careful consideration to everything that you will use during the ritual. Choose herbs and resins intuitively or by their scent, or opt for a ready-made blend that relaxes, calms, and grounds. Light the charcoal and wait for it to reach the correct heat. It can be helpful to describe each action aloud as you carry it out: "I am now lighting the charcoal," "I am placing the first portion of incense on the charcoal." When the incense begins to smolder, close your eyes and concentrate on the scent. Can you detect the fragrance of the different elements? Is the scent sweet or resinous, powerful or light? Does it change as the ritual progresses or stay the same? Think about its impact on your other senses. See the smoke as it curls and rises. Is it white and dense or thin? What sounds can you hear? The soft popping of lavender flowers in the heat, the hissing of melting resin? Feel the weight of the smudging bowl in your hands, the narrow handle of the spoon, the lightness of the air

and the slight resistance as you brush a feather through it. Your senses will transport you directly from your mind into your body, away from the past and future into the here and now, as the active substances in the herbs and resins bring relaxation.

When you feel calm and restored, complete the ritual by thanking the plants that have made themselves available to you (either aloud or silently). Let the charcoal burn out and drink a warm cup of tea to round off your smudging session.

Good Mood and Joy in Life

⇨ Blessing and Dedication ⇨ Energy and Vitality

NOTHING CAN put us in a bad mood more quickly than when we are brooding about something, whether it's a remark made by a work colleague, the state of our finances, or the grumpy person at the supermarket checkout—overthinking and holding on to negative emotions can easily spoil our day. Things are easier for animals in this respect, as anyone who has ever observed a dog that has had an unpleasant experience (being shouted at by a human or a disagreement with a nearby dog) will tell you. It knows how to shake it all off, quite literally, from its nose to the tip of its tail. This reduces the stress hormones and eases tension in the body, and good humor is restored. Like all animals, dogs live in the moment and don't waste time and energy on brooding over negative experiences. They rarely harbor resentment, while humans can, and do, routinely spoil their whole day by bearing a grudge.

However, it is easy to interrupt a downward spiral into negativity simply by reconnecting with your body. Many would find it difficult to stay in a bad mood when dancing to upbeat music, for example. A smudging session using a revitalizing or energizing scent, or just with a favorite fragrance is equally effective. Helped by the active substances in the incense, as soon as our attention is refocused on our body and our senses, intrusive thoughts become less important and fade into the background.

> Appropriate herbs and resins to promote good mood
> - bring light and sunshine to life;
> - give us confidence;
> - have a generally uplifting effect;
> - convey lightness and freshness;
> - energize and revitalize.
>
> **common:** birch, elecampane, hyssop, marigold, quince, rose, solidago, St John's wort, sweetgrass
> **exotic:** amber, copal (white and golden), mastic, myrrh

Add a touch of bright yellow to a smudging blend by including at least one flower with yellow petals in a selection of plants.

Incense blends designed to promote good mood are just as suitable as blends for a blessing, they help to energize and revitalize after a cleansing ritual (p. 38).

Smudging blends
Good mood
cedar, cinnamon, dammar gum, frankincense, ginger, rose, St John's wort
Well-being
copal (golden), lavender, quince, rose, styrax, sandalwood

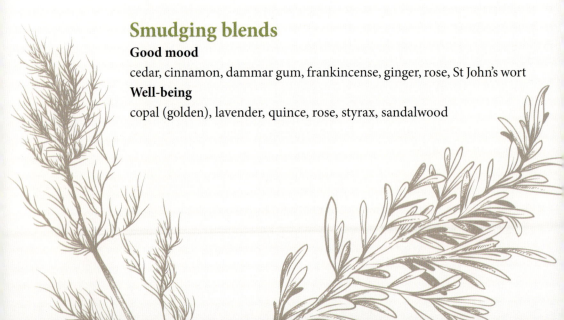

Grief and End-of-Life Care

⇨ Parting ⇨ Letting Go ⇨ Ancestors ⇨ Acceptance

SINCE DEATH HAS been removed from the family environment and banished to hospitals and hospices, and it is now the funeral home rather than relatives who wash and prepare a body for burial, death and dying have become a taboo subject. This does not mean that it has disappeared from our lives, of course. Instead, we are left to deal with death with no preparation or guidance. In the West we do not have the attitude to death that prevails in many cultures, where it is seen as a natural occurrence. Those who lose a loved one unexpectedly are left feeling just as bewildered and abandoned to the grieving process as those who have had to experience the slowly approaching death of someone seriously ill, being left to prepare as best they can with the resources at their disposal. We are also left helpless in the face of our own demise, lacking the words to express what is happening and what we are feeling. It is in such moments that rituals have their strength and power.

Herbs and resins suitable for sorrow and end-of-life care
- help us to let go and say farewell;
- warm and comfort us;
- bring inner peace;
- open up a path beyond the veil into the spirit world, making transition easier;
- bring light;
- help us to find the strength to endure the grieving process;
- help us to accept what has happened.

common: angelica, chamomile, daisy, elder, iris, juniper, lemon balm, marigold, meadowsweet, mugwort, rose, rosemary, Scots pine, spruce, St John's wort
exotic: benzoin, copal (black), cypress, frankincense, labdanum, myrtle

Plants that help us to deal with transition are particularly appropriate, not only making it easier for the deceased to cross to the other side, but also helping to unravel emotional entanglements.

Rosemary helps with grieving and letting go, angelica guides the deceased into the light, and elder resin eases transition for the dying. Cypress resin is also extremely useful, as it has an uplifting effect for the grieving. It grounds us, even when challenges seem unsurmountable, and helps us to process our emotions. Iris brings peace, acting like a protective shield, and soothes emotional tension.

Smudging blends
Inner peace (for sadness)
benzoin, cedar, frankincense
Saying farewell
angelica, elder, frankincense, mugwort, spruce, styrax

Grounding

⇨ Stress and Tension ⇨ Energy and Vitality ⇨ Letting Go

THE TERM grounding is much used. It can mean quite literally diverting an electric current to earth. This can be a natural electrical charge such as a bolt of lightning, or an electric current generated by a manmade device, such as in a short circuit or static charge. But grounding is good for us too when it means being in a position to deflect excess or external energies rather than allowing them to build up within us or diverting them out into the environment in an uncontrolled manner. In a metaphorical sense, grounding also helps us to gather our own energy and focus our thoughts when they are scattered and unclear. Grounding also describes the sense of a person being rooted or anchored. Our connection with the earth should not only be for channeling or diverting energy, but also for drawing on the energy of the planet, connecting us firmly with Mother Earth. Grounding therefore gives us a firm footing and a stable foundation on which to build our sense of self. We are at one with ourselves, something with which smudging can offer great support.

> Herbs and resins suitable for grounding
> - stabilize and center;
> - bring courage and confidence;
> - relax and calm the mind, helping us to be in the present moment;
> - make a connection with Mother Earth.
>
> **common:** angelica, fir, fumitory, juniper, larch, Scots pine, spruce
> **exotic:** agarwood, cedar, cypress, galbanum, guggul, labdanum, myrrh, opoponax, patchouli, sandalwood (white and red), vetiver

Smudging blends
Grounding I
angelica, cedar, myrrh, patchouli, sandalwood
Grounding II
frankincense, fumitory, labdanum, lavender, myrrh

Rituals
The mere act of smudging helps us to find calm and center ourselves, but if further grounding is needed, one of the following rituals may help.

Connecting with earth and sky
Choose a pleasant location, ideally outdoors or perhaps beside a window with a view of nature. You might also have a houseplant or a picture of a tree to help with the visualization part of this exercise. Prepare your smudging equipment, with everything readily to hand, and select some herbs and resins. Take a few breaths and say aloud or silently to yourself, "I am now completely centered." Light the charcoal and once it has

reached the correct heat, place the first portion of herbs and resins on top. Place the bowl on the floor and stand in front of it so that you are bathed in smoke from head to toe. Now visualize yourself as a tree.

See roots growing out of your feet and burrowing deep into the earth, holding and anchoring you. Spread out your arms and imagine them becoming the boughs of the tree, with branches full of blossom, leaves, and fruit. Feel the smoke rising up through your feet or your root chakra and into your body, and sense the earth nourishing and nurturing the tree. Feel how this energy flows upward, through your arms into your hands and fingertips, through your chest into your neck and head. Imagine water evaporating from the leaves, transferring energy into the air. Feel the warm rays of the sun shining down on you and a current of light and energy flowing down through the soles of your feet and into the earth. Just like a tree, you have now made a link between the sky above and the earth below.

The essence of a tree
The warm and earthy scents of domestic resinous trees in particular can help us to visualize ourselves as trees. If you have chosen tree resins for smudging, try the following ritual.

Breathe in the scent of the tree resins. Visualize standing in the middle of a forest as you take in the aromatic air. There are trees all around you. As in your mind's eye you look down upon yourself, you notice that you too have become a tree. Explore this feeling, rooted to this precise spot with your tree neighbors around you, standing under the same sun, for decades or even centuries. Feel the sense of peace and stability. There is nothing you have to do, nowhere you have to go, you have nothing to worry about, there are no to-do lists, your only obligation is to be here right now as a tree. Luxuriate in the feeling of being in exactly the right place and time, among your equals, an important part of the whole.

Headaches

HEADACHES CAN have a variety of triggers, and various medicinal plants can provide help, depending on the cause. Traditionally, they are generally used in teas (infusions) or are applied externally in a compress or as an oil. When used as incense in smudging, try holding a cotton or linen cloth in the smoke for a few seconds and then applying the cloth to the painful area (in this case, the temples).

> In general, any herb or resin that is relaxing and antispasmodic can be of help, but first make sure that you can tolerate odors during a migraine attack.
>
> **common:** angelica, birch, iris, lavender, lemon balm, meadowsweet, mint, mugwort, mullein, sage, solidago, St John's wort, yarrow
>
> **exotic:** cloves, frankincense, vetiver

Smudging blends

Headaches caused by weather sensitivity
lemon balm

Headaches due to liver disease
angelica, milk thistle

Tension headaches
mint, valerian

Relaxation
lavender, mugwort

Migraine
feverfew, iris, mullein, valerian, yarrow

Inhibit inflammation and relieve pain
frankincense, meadowsweet, willow bark

Healing

PROTECTION FROM (and the healing of) disease is one of the three major themes associated with smudging and incense traditions. In the past sickrooms and stalls for animals would all be fumigated on a regular basis, although it was carried out more as protection against witches and demons than against germs. However, smudging was also used to treat physical conditions, and some incense substances do indeed soothe physical complaints, while others boost the immune system or have analgesic or anti-inflammatory properties. Incense can alleviate symptoms on a physical level, as we know from the medicinal plants used in teas, tinctures, salves, and compresses, but they do not affect the body alone. Their influence on the mind and soul, and the body's ability to self-heal, is just as important, or even more so; what we believe and expect to happen often influences what is to come. A positive and optimistic doctor will heal more patients than one who habitually gives gloomy prognoses.

Healing does not always mean recovery to perfect health, however. Those who are at peace with what is, what has been, and what will come to pass have equally been healed.

> Herbs and resins that help with healing
> - soothe symptoms (for example, pain, circulatory complaints, and menstrual problems);
> - disinfect the air;
> - help us to accept a situation as it stands;
> - bring us lightness, confidence, and inner peace;
> - boost the immune system and the body's powers of self-healing.

The body

Even when the causes of complaints are unknown or are not yet diagnosed and so cannot be treated, we can still benefit from soothing the physical symptoms. See below for specific herbs and resins to ease certain conditions, and in addition the following conditions: respiratory problems (p. 92), headaches (p. 65), muscle tension and stiffness (p. 78), rheumatism (p. 94), women's issues (p. 97).

Herbs and resins

Stimulating the circulation (for low blood pressure): galangal, juniper, mint, mistletoe, rosemary, sage, thyme

Regulating the circulation (for high blood pressure): lavender, lemon balm

Strengthening the heart: cinnamon, lemon balm, marigold, Scots pine, tonka

Boosting the body's powers of self-healing and the immune system: angelica, chamomile, elder, masterwort, meadowsweet, mugwort, sage, sweetgrass, thyme

Pain relief: cloves, frankincense, iris, meadowsweet, myrtle, willow bark

Fighting infection: chamomile, elder, guggul, lavender, marigold, mint, myrrh, myrtle

Inhibiting inflammation: benzoin, chamomile, frankincense, guggul, larch, lavender, myrrh, oak, palo santo, sage, sandalwood (white)

Antibacterial/antiviral properties: benzoin, camphor, cardamom, cloves, cypress, eucalyptus, hyssop, juniper, larch, lavender, masterwort, meadowsweet, mullein, myrrh, oak, palo santo, rosemary, sage, solidago, spruce, sweetgrass, thyme

The mind

It is often the case that no specific root cause can be found for physical complaints. Sometimes this means that we need to look further for the cause, but equally it may mean that the cause is not somatic but rather that a sick or unhappy mind is affecting the body and is finding expression in physical symptoms.

Either way, it is worth performing a smudging ritual in which you can ask for a symbolic image of your condition. As all illness is caused by disruption to the flow of energy (such as the flow of blood to a part of the body being too strong or too weak, tissue that grows too much or too little), it can help to visualize this energy flow and so identify a symbolic clue to the cause.

Ritual
Visualizing vital energy

Take a moment to collect your thoughts and center yourself. Prepare your smudging equipment and choose the herbs and resins you wish to use. Blends that relax and promote meditation will be the most appropriate. Light the charcoal, and place the first portion of incense on top. Breathe in the scent and feel yourself slowly relaxing. Allow the scent of the incense to float down through your body. Now ask your soul for a symbolic image of your vital energy as it currently stands. An image may automatically appear in your mind's eye, but if not you might vizualize a garden, a house, a plant or a tree. Whatever comes to mind is a symbol of your being. Focus on the image. Is the garden well-kept or untidy? Does the plant or tree look healthy, or are the leaves wilting? Is the house neat, are the windows clean, has the driveway been swept, or are the trashcans overflowing? How does your ideal home, your ideal garden look? Do you see a lawn that needs to be mown or a wildflower meadow? Is it too dry or is it waterlogged? Do you see minimalist, sparsely furnished rooms, or rooms that are full of things, that look more lived in? There is no need to try and interpret what you see, simply begin by tending to your plant or tree, redesigning your house or garden, making changes until it feels good and right for you. When you feel as though you have reached the end of the ritual, let the charcoal burn down or extinguish it. Before relaxing fully, make a note of what you have seen and the changes you made. It is not necessary to understand the changes for them to work, but some link between what you see and what is troubling you will be obvious. For example, water that is still and does not flow represents stagnating vital energy, and clutter and dirt suggest that you should try a purification and detoxifying ritual. Repeat the ritual to see whether the changes that you visualized and/or have carried out in real life are reflected in your mental image. Do not forget to thank yourself for this valuable work.

Insect Repellent

NO ELABORATE ritual is required to repel insects, since certain herbs automatically have the effect of driving away flies, mosquitoes, moths, and wasps, just as does smoke. Tie bunches of the appropriate herbs or place suitable ground resin in small bags and hang them in your wardrobe or in a room. To keep flies away when outside, take advantage of a campfire to place incense on any pieces of wood or charcoal that are cooling down around the edges of the fire. Avoid placing any incense in the center of the wood or charcoal as it will simply burn without releasing any fragrance.

> **common:** lavender, lemon balm, mugwort
> **exotic:** bay leaf, camphor, cardamom, cedar, cinnamon, cloves, cypress, eucalyptus, patchouli, tonka, vetiver

Letting Go

⇨ Parting ⇨ Grief and End-of-Life Care ⇨ New Beginnings and Transition ⇨ Acceptance

THE ACT OF letting go is less immediate than saying goodbye, which always implies an ending, the idea that something is disappearing from our life, either irrevocably or at least for some time. It closes a chapter, it marks a turning point, something is ceasing or departing, something new is coming or beginning. Letting go can also mean loosening attachments, giving someone or something their freedom, as well as freeing ourselves from certain thoughts, attitudes, and habits. Letting go can occur at any time. It is when we decide to dismiss a certain thought from our mind, to allow a set of circumstances no further influence on our life, to pay no further attention to this or that feeling. We can shake off whatever has been concerning or affecting us, even if just for that moment.

> Herbs and resins that help us to let go
> - are relaxing;
> - have an easing and moderating effect;
> - open the heart;
> - ease stress and anxiety;
> - stop our thoughts from racing and allow us to take a breath.
>
> **common:** ash, lady's bedstraw, chamomile, elder, hops, iris, larch, lavender, meadowsweet, mugwort, rose, rosemary, solidago, spruce, sweetgrass, verbena, yarrow
> **exotic:** benzoin, cedar, dammar gum, guggul, opoponax, sandalwood (white), styrax, tonka

Smudging blends
Letting go I
guggul, labdanum, rose, styrax, sweetgrass, tonka
Letting go II
aniseed, bay leaf, calamus, chamomile, elder, marigold, mugwort, rose

Ritual
The following ritual may help to free you from certain thoughts, feelings, and beliefs.

Letting go of feelings
Take the time to gather your thoughts and center yourself in the present moment. Prepare your smudging equipment. Make a note of what you would like to release on a piece of paper. Think about what thoughts and emotions—fear of change, loneliness, or the future, perhaps anger at friends or work colleagues, or the mountain of laundry waiting for you at home—you wish to let go. If there are several, write each one down on a separate piece of paper.

When you are ready, light the charcoal. Once it has reached the correct heat, place the first portion of herbs and resins on top. Breathe in the scent and think about how you are feeling. Place the first scrap of paper and another portion of incense on the charcoal. Watch the paper burn and visualize the energies it represents melting away at the same time. It may help to say aloud, "I now release my feeling of . . . ."

Sorrow, fear, uncertainty, rage, envy . . . all these negative emotions can be burned away with incense. Place each successive scrap of paper and a portion of incense on the charcoal in turn. When you have finished, think again about how you are feeling. Is there anything else within you that you would still like to release. When you feel that the ritual has come to an end, complete it by finally adding a smudging blend for a blessing. Now relax and thank yourself for having had the courage to perform this ritual.

Light-Bringers

⇨ Energy and Vitality ⇨ Courage and Self-Confidence ⇨ Good Mood and Joy in Life ⇨ Blessing and Consecration ⇨ Annual Festivals

LIGHT-BRINGER describes plants that are in flower on and around the summer solstice. They store the healing power of the sun in their (often yellow) petals and flowers. This power can then be released in winter in the form of incense used in smudging (in particular on the winter solstice or during the nights of the yuletide season). Light-bringing plants have the power to brighten our mood, to drive away cares and sorrows, and fill us with vitality. They are often found in blends that are intended to bring about good mood, and to encourage and energize us. Light-bringing herbs are also suitable for use in blessings and charging a cleansed room with good energy.

common: angelica, chamomile, elecampane, marigold, meadowsweet, solidago, St John's wort, sweetgrass
exotic: amber, dammar gum, mastic, styrax

Love and Sensuality

⇨ Stress and Tension ⇨ Acceptance ⇨ Women's Issues

IF TAROT CARDS could speak, they would tell us that practically every question they are asked falls into one of three categories: health, money... but above all, love. While we ask such questions more out of curiosity than anything else, they were very important for our ancestors, so it is little wonder that practically all folk customs and superstitions have something to do with these three themes. Love oracles are the most common: the woman who catches the bride's bouquet (or the man who catches the garter) will be the next to marry, the face seen in dreams on Christmas Eve or New Year's Eve belongs to your future partner, and so on.

Some of the love charms and spells handed down over the generations involve incense. While the love potions that appear in fantasy literature, from *A Midsummer Night's Dream* to the Harry Potter books, take possession of the bewitched person against their conscious will, smudging used to attract someone romantically works in a different way. In this case, the aim is to create an atmosphere that makes it easier for partners to engage with their feelings as well as with one another. Some of the plants used (roses, for example) have an effect through their symbolic power alone, while it is the enchanting scent of others, such as patchouli, that enhances the mood. Just as our body odor is dependent on our state of mind and hormone levels, scents can influence our emotional state and physiology. It therefore comes as no surprise to learn that phytohormones and substances that affect hormones have been discovered in several of the herbs and resins traditionally used for romantic purposes.

> Herbs and resins suitable for smudging for romance
> - open the heart and help those taking part to engage with themselves and with their partner;
> - dissolve emotional blockages;
> - create a romantic mood and a sensual atmosphere;
> - balance hormones or guide them in the right direction;
> - are physically and mentally relaxing, as stress is the greatest killer of desire.
>
> **common:** lady's bedstraw, birch, daisy, hops, lady's mantle, meadowsweet, quince, rose, rosemary, solidago, sweetgrass
> **exotic:** agarwood, benzoin, cardamom, cinnamon, cloves, copaiba, guggul, labdanum, myrtle, patchouli, sandalwood, styrax, tonka, vetiver

Rosemary has long been a universal presence in love charms. It has an aphrodisiac, sensual, and stimulating effect and opens the heart. Lady's mantle can be burned on its own in smudging for romantic purposes. When placed under the pillow, sweetgrass is said to awaken desire, while solidago can help to heal a relationship. Guggul has a balancing effect, creating a harmonious atmosphere and cleansing a room after an argument (this also applies in the workplace and at family events).

Smudging blends
Living with love
cardamom, elder, juniper, mastic, rose, sandalwood (red), thyme
Night of love
lady's mantle, meadowsweet, myrtle, rose, styrax
Sensuality
benzoin, iris, lavender, myrtle, quince, rose, rosemary, styrax
Eroticism
benzoin, labdanum, lady's bedstraw, meadowsweet, myrtle, quince, styrax, tonka

Aphrodisiac
asafetida, cinnamon, guggul, rose, rosemary, sandalwood (red and white), styrax, vetiver

Rituals

We are our own worst enemies when it comes to affairs of the heart, something that is equally true whether we are looking for a partner or trying to maintain an existing relationship, and it also applies to our sexual lives. That is why the first step when dealing with problems of a romantic nature is to come to terms with our own feelings, attitudes, and emotional blockages.

Developing self-love
Take a little time-out for yourself and your relationships. Self-care is the first step toward self-acceptance. Begin by preparing the room—it should be somewhere that you won't be disturbed. Prepare your equipment and select your incense ingredients or choose a ready-made blend, some relaxing, calming, and comforting herbs and resins that will open your heart. You might like to place nearby a few items that remind you of some of your favorite people or things: a plant, a vase of flowers, a soft toy, or a photograph of your parents, children, or pets.

When you are ready, light the charcoal, wait until it reaches the correct heat, and place the first portion of incense on top. Breathe in the smoke, and feel it permeating you and touching your heart. Now imagine how, together with the fragrance, love flows into you, penetrating not just your physical body but your spiritual bodies too. How do you feel? Are there any parts of you where the smoke and love cannot penetrate?

Revel in this fragrance and see how those hard-to-reach parts of you soften. Breathe in the fragrance and imagine breathing out whatever is causing a blockage and seeing it dissolve. This may take some time, but allowing yourself this time is a sign of self-love. If any blockages or troublesome emotions refuse to dissolve, say aloud or silently to yourself, "I accept you. I see you. I love myself as I am." When you are as filled with love as you can be, thank yourself and thank the plants that have helped you. If the charcoal is still sufficiently hot, you may like to add a blend for a blessing. Now bring the ritual to an end; it can be repeated as required.

Ritual for couples

Allow yourselves some time together as a couple for this ritual. Choose somewhere that feels peaceful and welcoming. Prepare your smudging equipment and pay close attention to choosing your blend. You might like to do this together, choosing scents that appeal to you both, or take turns to select herbs and resins. If you decide to use a ready-prepared mixture, ideally choose one that contains both male-associated and female-associated aromas, such as rose and cedar.

Light the charcoal, and when it has reached the required heat, place the incense on top. Begin with either you or your partner holding the smudging bowl between you at heart level. Breathe in the scent of the burning herbs. You may like to say a few words about what you particularly appreciate in your partner or what you would like from them. One of you should now cup some of the smoke in your hands and use it to bathe the whole of your partner's body, working gradually, from the soles of their feet to the top of their head. Focus on each part of the body for as long as feels right and good. Now add some more of the incense to the charcoal and swap roles. Visualize the smoke carrying away all the disruptive energies, cleansing you within, and enveloping you both in a light-filled cloud.

Allow the charcoal to burn down. Whether you bring the ritual to a close by relaxing together or with some other activity is of course entirely up to you.

Meditation and Inner Vision

⇨ Prayer and Invocation ⇨ Clarity

SINCE YOGA, meditation, and the burning of incense sticks (often loaded with patchouli) were introduced from India to the West by the 1960s hippy movement, they are now all almost indelibly linked in the minds of many. Burning incense for sacred purposes (including inner vision and reflection) is indeed an ancient and almost universal practice. There is barely a temple or religion that does not use or have recourse to sacred smoke. In the past the incense would often contain a range of hallucinogenic plants that would induce deep trances, unleashing a flood of images. Nowadays, when many traditional ceremonies and rites have been forgotten or lost and there are no experienced priests or shamans to guide us (or at least rarely so), the use of specifically psychoactive herbs and resins cannot be recommended. Nonetheless, sufficient plants do exist that are less harmful and make it easier for us to enter a contemplative state or fall into a trance so that we can find peace and be open to receiving inner images.

Herbs and resins encourage meditation if they
- calm the mind;
- relax the body and muscles;
- refresh the mind and "lend it wings;"
- open up the subconscious.

common: chamomile, elecampane, iris, mint, mugwort, mullein, rose, Scots pine, verbena

exotic: agarwood, bay leaf, camphor, cedar, copal (white), dammar gum, elemi, frankincense, guggul, gum arabic, labdanum, mastic, myrtle, opoponax, palo santo, patchouli, sandalwood (white), sandarac, spikenard

When meditating, avoiding scents that are physically stimulating or are particularly heavy and intense (such as patchouli) is recommended, but experiment and see what works for you. White sandalwood is one scent that most people seem able to tolerate quite well. Remember that our bodies can become accustomed and conditioned to certain things. Once you have found an incense fragrance or a blend that you find pleasant, it makes sense to keep using it. You will soon associate the fragrance with a meditative state of mind so that even simply smelling the incense will put you in the right frame of mind for the meditation to come.

Smudging blends
Meditation, domestic
elder, chamomile, lavender, rose, Scots pine, styrax, sweetgrass
Meditation, exotic
benzoin, cedar, frankincense, gum arabic, vetiver

Muscle Tension and Stiffness

ACTIVITIES THAT use only certain parts of the body, resulting in the overuse of certain muscles, and (in particular) long hours of sitting in unhealthy postures, have made muscle tension and stiffness a widespread problem that is only compounded by inner tension and stress. If stiffness and tension last for a long time, people tend to adopt postures that try to relieve them, leading to uneven wear and tear on the joints. Orthopedic practitioners often recommend building up muscle in the gym, but it is difficult to strengthen muscles that are tense as they become even more tense and stiff when subjected to stress. Relaxation should therefore be the first option, in addition to stretching exercises, yoga, or any form of natural movement, combined with heat treatment, ointments, and massage with essential oils. Smudging combines the healing powers of plants with warmth—don't simply breathe in the smoke, bathe your whole body in it.

If stiffness and tension are severe, a smudging chair/stool can be used (as recommended for rheumatism). A smudging bowl is placed beneath the central part of the seat, which contains an opening so that the smoke from the incense can rise up through the opening. Wrap yourself in a blanket and your whole body will be warmed by the smoke. A cloth can also be bathed in and infused with the smoke and then applied to tense muscles. Try also bathing the reflex zones on the hands and feet in the smoke of incense.

> Herbs and resins that ease muscle tension
> - stimulate blood flow;
> - have a warming effect;
> - have a relaxing effect.
>
> **common:** chamomile, hops, larch, lavender, mugwort, rosemary, Scots pine, St John's wort, verbena
> **exotic:** camphor, cinnamon, cloves, cypress, ginger, palo santo

Smudging blends
Relaxation for the body
frankincense, hops, lavender, mastic, rosemary

New Beginnings and Transition

⇨ Parting ⇨ Letting Go ⇨ Women's Issues

NEW BEGINNINGS and leave-taking are inextricably linked. While a farewell ritual emphasizes sorrow and loss, and is about closing the door on something, a ritual of new beginning celebrates the adventure of the new and welcomes us to the next chapter in our lives. With a new beginning, the emphasis is on joy, hope, and confidence. Smudging rituals can be used to accompany any transitional phase: changing job or school, moving house, the coming of age, or starting retirement. Crossing thresholds such as these is a natural part of the cycle of life, and all cultures have specific and significant rituals to accompany them. Added to these are those moments that we mark with a big celebration—think of weddings, baptisms, and so on, and in some cultures the initiation ceremonies in which boys are admitted among the ranks of the men and girls join the circle of women.

Herbs and resins suitable for celebrating and supporting new beginnings or transitions
- bring courage and confidence;
- energize and strengthen;
- make us happy and cheerful;
- help us to open up and be approachable;
- ground us and provide stability;
- provide a blessing for the new chapter in our life.

common: ash, birch, elecampane, hops, hyssop, iris, juniper, lady's mantle, lavender, larch, meadowsweet, mint, mugwort, oak, quince, rosemary, solidago, verbena, yarrow
exotic: agarwood, aniseed, bay leaf, cedar, cedar (American), copal (golden), dammar gum, elemi, myrrh, palo santo, sage (white), sandalwood (white)

Smudging blends

Inner freedom and new energy
frankincense, licorice, menthol, mugwort, myrrh, orange, rose, sandalwood, verbena
Self-confidence and self-assurance
benzoin, dammar gum, elecampane, mugwort, rose
New beginnings
benzoin, cedar, cedar (American), cinnamon, copal (golden), elder

Ritual
Breaking new ground

Begin the ritual by grounding and centering yourself. Prepare your utensils and choose the herbs and resins you wish to use. If not using a ready-made blend, think about what qualities or attributes you would like to take you through the next stage in your life—perhaps courage and self-confidence, or luck and success in achieving something—and choose the ingredients accordingly. You might like to place two pieces of fabric side by side or lay out a scarf horizontally in front of you to represent your transition from one life stage to the next.

Now light the charcoal and when it has reached the correct heat, place the first portion of herbs and resins on top. Hold the bowl in your hands and breathe in the smoke. As you do so, feel how new courage, confidence, belief in yourself and the future, or excitement about the adventure to come flow through you. Be fully aware of the floor in front of you and stand on the first piece of fabric or just in front of the line now formed by the scarf. This is your current situation or position in life. Think about how you currently feel about things.

When you are ready, take a bold and resolute step across onto the second piece of fabric or over the scarf. You might like to say aloud or silently to yourself, "I am leaving the old behind me and am now starting afresh, full of confidence." Breathe in the smoke from the incense and allow its energy to flood into this new situation. Welcome yourself and your new place in life. If you wish, ask for a blessing. Thank yourself for your courage, and finish the ritual as usual by allowing the charcoal to burn down and relaxing.

The Nights of Yuletide

⇨ Annual Festivals ⇨ Divination and Clairvoyance ⇨ Ancestors

DEPENDING ON the tradition, the nights of Yuletide extend from either the winter solstice (December 21) or Christmas Day (December 25) until Epiphany on January 6. This period, and especially the solstice, has a special significance in most cultures. Among the Germanic peoples and those of Northern Europe, the solstice was celebrated either as Julfest, Yul, or Midwinter. In Christianity, Christmas, the night of the birth of Christ, coincides with the old Roman festival honoring the sun god Sol Invictus. In Central Asia and Iran, the festival of Yalda Night is celebrated, while the Hindus of India and Nepal observe Makar Sankrati. What all these feast days have in common is that they celebrate the return of the light, even though the coldest and hardest part of the winter is still to come. The nights of Yuletide are therefore a time of hope and an anticipation of brighter days.

Certain people can sense that the veil between this world and the other world (or the unconscious) is thinner than usual at this time of year and that the threshold can be crossed more easily—for those on both sides. Just as subtle beings find it easier to cross over to our world (think of the Wild Hunt of Wotan, Odin in Norse tradition, and the goddess who roams the underworld as Hel or Percht), it is a time when it is easier to make contact with our ancestors or divine beings on the other side. It is in any case a time to draw a line under the old and consider what we would like to take with us into the new year, what new things we would like to begin, what new attitudes we would like to adopt, and what light we carry within us.

Herbs and resins suitable for the nights of Yuletide
- open up the threshold to the unconscious;
- help us to let go of the old and embrace brave new beginnings;
- cleanse;
- bring light into the darkest season;
- are made into herb bundles;
- help us to glimpse the future (divination).

common: angelica, chamomile, fir, juniper, larch, masterwort, mistletoe, mugwort, sage, Scots pine, spruce, St John's wort, sweetgrass, yarrow

exotic: bay leaf, camphor, frankincense, myrrh, myrtle, styrax

Smudging blends
Nights of Yuletide
angelica, juniper, lavender, mugwort, myrtle, rosemary, sage (white), spruce (resin), verbena
Christmas
cinnamon, myrrh, palo santo, spruce (needles), tonka

Rituals
Much like spring, the period before Christmas (known as Advent) is a time when people like to clean their homes thoroughly, and it is always a nice idea to combine this with a smudging ritual.

Cleansing and blessing every space
Begin by grounding and centering yourself in whatever way is best for you. Prepare your smudging equipment and choose an incense blend, either one ready-made or by selecting ingredients intuitively. Ingredients that bring blessings can be added to those for cleansing. Once the charcoal has reached the correct heat, add the first portion of incense. Hold the smudging bowl level with your heart and inhale the scent. Choose an intention or affirmation and say it aloud or silently to yourself; for example, "Everything old that is of no further use must leave the room, now."

Take the smudging bowl through the house, room by room, and fan the smoke into each corner. Trust your instinct, some areas may feel denser and darker than others and the way the smoke rises might change. Continue the ritual for as long as feels right. You might like to repeat your intention silently, like a mantra or prayer. If the room feels empty, think about a second intention, such as "May light and love/blessings/happiness and fulfillment enter this room, now," and fill the cleansed room with good energy. Depending on the time available and the incense selected, you may now wish to carry out a blessing ritual.

It is advisable to open a window, even if only during the cleansing ritual, so that the old energy can escape along with the smoke. Once all the rooms have been cleansed and blessed, thank the plants that have made themselves available to you. If you wish, an energy spray or a spritz of water can now be used to bind the smoke particles floating in the air.

Looking ahead to the coming year
The nights of Yuletide are traditionally a time for looking into the future. Energies are reorganized and it is easier than usual to look over the threshold and into what is to come. Many customs have come down to us from our ancestors: evergreen plants such as firs and holly are cut and brought into the home, symbolizing life, renewal, and hope for the future, and bells are rung to drive away evil spirits and herald the lighter days that will ultimately follow the solstice.

Other options for looking into the future at this time of the year include
- keeping a dream diary (a smudging session to promote dreams may help you to have more lucid dreams and to remember them more clearly);
- being aware of any signs and portents around you; this could be anything from an advertising billboard that catches your eye, a passing remark, or an animal that crosses your path;
- drawing tarot cards for the year to come or picking a card on each night of Yuletide for the successive months of the coming year; a smudging ritual for divination (p. 49) can also help with this.

Parting

⇨ Grief and End-of-Life Care ⇨ Letting Go ⇨ Acceptance
⇨ New Beginnings and Transition

FORMS OF PARTING and taking leave of something range from those that are small and temporary, such as when a family member goes to work or school in the morning, to major and life-changing events such as when a marriage falls apart. We also say goodbye to houses and locations when we move, to jobs and colleagues during our careers, even to friends when we grow apart. We also leave behind favorite (but perhaps not healthy) habits and phases of life. The most profound parting we experience is when we lose a loved one (addressed in more detail in Grief and End-of-Life Care, p. 61). What all these forms of parting have in common, however, is that we are leaving behind something familiar and crossing a threshold to something new.

A smudging session to bid farewell can help us to open the door and step over this threshold to meet the new with courage and confidence. It will also help us to let go. In both pharmacological and physical terms, smudging can relieve the inner stress and tension experienced when we fight change. This kind of smudging session can revitalize and bring confidence, giving us cause for optimism.

Herbs and resins suitable for a smudging session to say goodbye to someone or something

- bring us energy, courage, and confidence;
- reduce stress and bring inner peace;
- help us to accept our own feelings;
- are calming and relaxing.

common: angelica, elder, iris, juniper, meadowsweet, mugwort, rosemary, spruce, Scots pine, yarrow
exotic: benzoin, cedar, cypress, sandalwood, spikenard, styrax

Smudging blends
Inner peace
benzoin Sumatra, cinnamon, lavender, orange, rose, styrax, tonka
Inner freedom and new energy
frankincense, licorice, mugwort, myrrh, rose, sandalwood, verbena
Promoting contact with ancestors
angelica, elder, frankincense, juniper, mugwort, spruce (resin)

Rituals
Memorial altar
When having to say farewell to a loved one or a pet, making a small (and perhaps temporary) altar can help. It might contain a photograph and object with which you associate the departed. Light a candle in their honor and burn either a comforting, warming smudging blend or choose one with the departed's favorite scent. Be mindful of your sorrow, but also think about all the memories in which the person (or animal) lives on within you. Thank them for their existence and for all the gifts they gave you. You may sense when the time is right for you to let the departed pass on.

If a little more support is needed to help process loss, or if you wish to actively organize a process of saying goodbye, try the following ritual.

Actively bidding farewell
Prepare the equipment needed for the session and perhaps light a candle. Take a moment to collect and center yourself in the present moment. On a small scrap of paper, write down what you wish to let go or to what you wish to—or have to—say goodbye. Alternatively, you might like to consider which of your thoughts and feelings (for example, fear of change, loneliness, or of the future in general) you wish to leave behind and make a note of these on a small piece of paper. Think about where these emotions are anchored within you; you might see them as dark or dense places, or as a mental image of a stone or a thorn.

When you are ready, light the charcoal. As soon as it has reached the correct heat, place the first portion of incense on top. Inhale the scent and visualize it penetrating your being and slowly dissolving the dense, dark places. Imagine the energies released by the smoke being carried away into the sky. Now add the piece of paper to the charcoal (with the note of what you wish to let go), and add more herbs and resins on top of this. Imagine your thoughts and emotional pain evaporating. It might help to affirm aloud, "I am letting my feeling of … rise into the sky with this smoke." The sorrow, fear, and uncertainty will rise with the smoke, leaving behind a fresh and empty space that can now be filled with something new. Finish the session by placing a blend of herbs and resins that brings blessings on the charcoal or simply choose those that you most enjoy using.

Prayer and Invocation

⇨ Meditation and Inner Vision ⇨ Blessing and Consecration

PRAYER AND INVOCATION are closely connected with meditation and sacrificial offering. In many cultures it is believed that smoke can carry prayers and songs, enabling people to make contact with the gods or their ancestors. While a prayer embodies a request or an expression of gratitude to a divinity or spiritual helper (often in a set form), invocation goes a step further and can be understood as a direct appeal to the divine to act on behalf of or through the individual, or even to appear in person.

Each culture had its own temple incense that would accompany its sacred rites and ceremonies. Much of the Western Christian world associates the smell of incense with the church and divine services, and even those who don't feel particularly drawn to Christianity can sense the transcendent, otherworldly nature of old cathedrals. It is not too difficult to imagine that particular divinities can be contacted through certain scents, as all incense substances essentially have psychoactive properties. This is why when in a sacred place or performing a ritual, we enter an altered state of consciousness in which the location, the scent we perceive, and the rituals we carry out combine to make it easy to open ourselves up to prayer and the spirit world.

> Herbs and resins suitable for prayer and invocation
> - are traditionally associated with a particular divinity;
> - open us up to the spirit world;
> - summon spirit helpers;
> - calm and/or focus thoughts.
>
> **common:** fumitory, iris, oak, spruce, verbena
> **exotic:** agarwood, amber, benzoin, camphor, cedar, cedar American), copal (white), dammar gum, elemi, frankincense, guggul, mastic, myrtle, nutmeg

Some herbs and resins are said to open up a connection to our spirit helpers (iris), to the divine (white copal), angels (dammar gum), nature spirits (thyme), and elves (fumitory).

Smudging blends
Entering light-filled worlds
angelica, damiana, dammar gum, frankincense, hyssop, rose, styrax
Recognizing your own divine light
angelica, cedar, copal, juniper, frankincense, myrrh, opoponax, St John's wort
Blessing
elecampane, frankincense, juniper, mugwort, myrrh, styrax, sandalwood (white)

Protection

⇨ Cleansing

ALONG WITH CLEANSING, smudging for protection is one of the oldest uses of the smoke generated by incense. In the eyes of our ancestors, everything from the family and livestock to the crops and harvest had to be protected from witchcraft, demons, and the evil eye in order to ensure survival. Today we know that many of the plants traditionally used to cleanse and protect in smudging rituals possess active disinfectant and antiseptic substances.

This use of incense can also work on an invisible, subtle level by removing low-vibrating external energies and influences or shielding us from their effects. Workers in an open-plan office can shield themselves and their own aura to ensure that no negative surrounding energies—stress, dissatisfaction, the anxieties of colleagues—can affect them.

When we cleanse ourselves, we remove any external energies or harmful bacteria that are present. When we protect ourselves, we create a shield, a barrier against external energies or pathogens. During the Covid-19 pandemic, we disinfected our hands to get rid of viruses and wore face coverings as a means of protection. It therefore makes sense to cleanse first and then to protect the cleansed areas from further contamination. With regard to disease, strengthening the immune system also forms part of protection.

> Herbs and resins suitable for smudging for protection purposes
> - strengthen our energy field;
> - clear the atmosphere;
> - help us to focus on ourselves;
> - have considerable light power (herbs of the sun).
>
> **common:** angelica, ash, elder, fumitory, juniper, lavender, marigold, masterwort, meadowsweet, mistletoe, mugwort, rosemary, rue, sage, Scots pine, St John's wort, verbena
> **exotic:** amber, bay leaf, calamus, cypress, dammar gum, dragon's blood, myrrh, opoponax, palo santo

Some herbs and resins are also suitable for smudging for protection: myrrh acts like a protective cloak against external energies, while palo santo stabilizes the aura and fills the energy field with good energies; in the Catholic areas of the Alps, bay leaves are traditionally burned at Epiphany to ward off dark forces; and lavender helps to protect women (especially younger women) during menstruation.

Substances that smell bad to evil spirits and drive them away are often less than agreeable to our own noses too. Some herbs, such as fumitory, that are particularly effective when used for protection and cleansing have a rather unpleasant smell.

Smudging blends

Protection, domestic ingredients
ash, juniper, mistletoe, mugwort, spruce, verbena

Protection and strength
amber, dragon's blood, juniper, verbena

Power and support
angelica, dragon's blood, juniper, mugwort, olibanum, sandalwood (white)

Ritual

The method used in a cleansing ritual (p. 38) can be followed in a simple protection ritual as well. Imagine the smoke rising to form a protective shield or cloak around you or indeed the whole the room. Negative energies will simply bounce off this protective shell.

Respiratory Problems

THERE IS A long tradition, all over the world, of burning combinations of herbs to treat breathing problems. What might at first sound counterproductive (how can you breathe more easily in air filled with smoke?) actually has medicinal benefits. Many of the herbs used in traditional treatments have disinfectant and antiseptic properties and so provide protection, not just to the person suffering from respiratory problems, but to all those in the room or space where the smudging is being carried out.

Once inhaled, medicinal herbs continue to work in the nose, throat, and lungs. The smoke helps to loosen mucus so that it can be expelled more easily through coughing, blood flow to the lungs is stimulated, and constricted bronchial tubes expand. In the early 20th century, so-called "asthma cigarettes" containing coltsfoot, along with well-known ingredients such as hemp or toxic but highly effective thorn apple, were sold to provide relief to sufferers.

> Useful herbs and resins for respiratory issues include those that
> - strengthen the lungs;
> - loosen phlegm and help it to be expelled through coughing;
> - restrict mucilage and so reduce a tickle in the throat;
> - have general antiseptic properties.
>
> **common:** angelica, elder, elecampane, fir, hyssop, juniper, larch, mullein, rosemary, sage, Scots pine, spruce, thyme
> **exotic:** agarwood, bay leaf, benzoin, cedar (American), copaiba, cypress, eucalyptus, galangal, myrrh, myrtle, styrax

Smudging blends

Loosen thick phlegm, chronic complaints, and stubborn infections
angelica, elecampane, hyssop, larch, thyme

Dry or chesty cough, improving oxygen intake
mullein, Scots pine

Productive cough, runny nose
elder, sage

Unproductive cough with mucus in the lungs
birch, hyssop, thyme

Asthma, whooping cough
agarwood, coltsfoot, elder, elecampane, mugwort, sage, St John's wort, thyme

Rheumatism

⇨ Muscle Tension ⇨ Headaches

RHEUMATISM IS GENERALLY seen as a disease of the joints that primarily affects older people. However, it is in fact an umbrella term for a wide range of conditions affecting the musculoskeletal system: the joints and articular capsules, muscles, tendons, sinews, bones, but also connective tissue and blood vessels. The causes vary, including inflammation, auto-immune disease, and pain from wear and tear. Medicinal plants can help to bring relief.

> Depending on the cause, herbs and resins that can help rheumatism
> - boost blood flow;
> - relax the muscles;
> - stimulate the circulation (along with kidney and liver function) and so help to remove toxins;
> - have anti-inflammatory properties;
> - have analgesic properties;
> - have antidepressant properties.
>
> **common:** ash, hyssop, juniper, lavender, marigold, meadowsweet, mint, mistletoe, solidago, spruce, willow bark
> **exotic:** agarwood, frankincense, guajak, guggul

A traditional healing technique that can be used to treat rheumatism is to use a smudging chair or stool (p. 79). The patient is covered with a blanket or cloth to capture the warmth and active substances contained in the smoke. A blend of lavender, frankincense, and mastic is used, although frankincense, whose effects have been confirmed in studies, can also be used alone. A smudging cloth—a cotton or linen cloth infused with smoke from the incense and used as an overlay or compress—may also be of help.

Stress and Tension

⇨ Fear and Anxiety ⇨ Letting Go ⇨ Evening Smudging Session

STRESS IS PROBABLY the most serious and common side effect of our modern lifestyle. Flooded with information from our smartphones and the internet, and weighed down with lengthy to-do lists and appointment schedules that are bursting at the seams, we find it difficult to find any peace. We are permanently on call and even our favorite pastimes (computer games or watching TV, perhaps), which may seem to relax us, don't really bring fulfillment—quite the opposite, in fact, they only make the burden worse. And even as our minds are whirling, our bodies are often neglected or overly stressed. Long hours of sitting coupled with too little exercise means we lose muscle and our joints seize up, causing pain and tension that only serves to raise our general stress levels even further.

Apart from switching off the various screens that constantly surround us, one thing will do us more good than anything else—to get out into nature. Exercise in the fresh air helps to reduce excess adrenaline levels and to strengthen the muscles, but most importantly the scents of nature—of the earth beneath our feet and of plants and trees in particular—also help to calm the mind. Scientific studies have now shown just how much a stroll in woodland can be of benefit. It is no coincidence that forest bathing has been part of the public health service in Japan since the 1980s. Not everyone is lucky enough to live right next to a forest or is able to access one, however, in which case smudging can offer a wonderful alternative.

Any domestic tree that produces resin (especially conifer resin) can be used to bring the scent of the forest into the home.

Herbs and resins that help with stress
- relax us physically;
- focus the mind and calm the nerves;
- help us to feel at one with nature;
- have a grounding effect (p. 62).

common: lady's bedstraw, chamomile, elecampane, hops, larch, lavender, lemon balm, Scots pine, spruce, St John's wort, sweetgrass, valerian, yarrow
exotic: aniseed, benzoin, calamus, cedar, cinnamon, copaiba, copal (golden), galbanum, guggul, myrrh, opoponax, palo santo, patchouli, sandalwood, sandarac, styrax, tonka

Smudging blends
Pure relaxation
benzoin, copal, lavender, rose, sandalwood (white), styrax
Inner peace
benzoin Sumatra, cinnamon, orange, lavender, rose, styrax, tonka

Women's Issues

OUR ANCESTORS were familiar with certain herbs that were particularly suitable for helping women and young girls, so these were also typically used for women's rituals.

Girls

A number of plants can help to ease a girl's path to becoming a woman. One such plant is meadowsweet (another name is bridewort and it would often be found in a bride's bouquet). Much like birch, meadowsweet is a plant of new beginnings and therefore it is a good ritual plant for soothing a girl's first menstruation.

Lavender provides protection from "energy vampires" (people who drain our energy) during menstruation and at times of anxiety and uncertainty about the opposite sex and our own sexuality.

> Young women may be helped by herbs and resins that
> - boost feelings of self-worth and self-love;
> - help us to accept our own body and all the changes it undergoes;
> - ease transition, in this instance leaving behind girlhood and welcoming the transition to adulthood as a woman;
> - deflect outside energies.
>
> **common:** birch, chamomile, daisy, elder, lavender, meadowsweet
> **exotic:** myrrh, myrtle

Regulating menstruation

Some traditional herbs used for smudging to treat menstrual disorders, cramps, and symptoms of menopause contain certain hormone-like substances. Examples include hops and lavender, which contain phytoestrogens, and lady's mantle, which contains phytoprogestins.

> Herbs and resins that help to regulate menstruation: chamomile, chasteberry, hops, lady's mantle, lavender, meadowsweet, mugwort, St John's wort, thyme, yarrow

Midwifery

Childbirth and the period immediately following it was a perilous time for our ancestors, both for the mother and for the child. To protect from demons, witches, and general misfortune, expectant mothers would be laid upon mattresses stuffed with straw and herbs. The herbs often contained large quantities of essential oils and coumarin and so could offer some protection by warding off germs. Chasteberry and/or lady's bedstraw were more usually placed in the beds of young women, as they are said to help promote chastity and lower the libido. Other herbs known to have been used in childbirth include chamomile, lady's bedstraw, lady's mantle, mugwort, St John's wort, sweetgrass, wild thyme, valerian, and woodruff. Lavender, thyme, and rosemary were also used postpartum, and all these herbs were used as incense ingredients. In the past some herbs and resins and/or medicinal plants (such as mugwort, galbanum, and labdanum) that encourage birth and induce labor were also used to induce abortion, as they accelerate labor and promote the expulsion of the placenta. All such herbs and resins should be avoided during pregnancy in order to help reduce the risk of miscarriage.

Held in the left hand during birth, mugwort in particular is said to speed and ease delivery and ensure a good outcome. Moxibustion or moxa therapy, in which smoldering rolls of mugwort (known as moxa sticks) are held against particular acupuncture points, is a technique used when preparing for birth, such as to turn the baby in the event of an abnormal position, for example. However, if intending to use herbs and resins as incense for smudging (or in any other way) during childbirth, always consult with your doctor or midwife first.

Myrrh oil was traditionally used to disinfect the perineum and make it supple. It would also be applied as a disinfectant to the umbilical stump of the newborn's navel. Myrrh was also used to help prepare for and ease birth. It would be smoked over hot coals that were placed under the birthing stool.

> Herbs and resins that ease birth
> - strengthen the organs of the pelvis;
> - promote birth and induce labor;
> - have disinfectant and antiseptic properties;
> - have a relaxing and calming effect.
>
> **common:** lady's bedstraw, birch, chamomile, chasteberry, daisy, hops, lady's mantle, lavender, rosemary, St John's wort, sweetgrass, thyme, wild thyme, valerian, woodruff, yarrow
> **exotic:** myrrh, myrtle

Glossary of
HERBS & RESINS

This section lists a comprehensive selection of herbs and resins with all their essential attributes. When buying incense, always make sure it is of good quality since the smoke will automatically be inhaled during a smudging ritual.

With some plants commonly used for smudging, it is advisable to use only small amounts (a three-finger pinch). The glossary gives details of the herbs and resins to which this applies (such as mistletoe and tonka).

The following herbs and resins should form an essential part of your starter pack of incense ingredients.

Resins and balms: benzoin, copal, dammar gum, frankincense, mastic, myrrh, Scots pine, spruce, styrax

Herbs, woods, roots, and flowers: angelica, bay leaf, calamus, cedar, cinnamon, juniper, lavender, mugwort, myrtle, patchouli, rose, rosemary, sage, sandalwood, spruce

Agarwood

Name:	*Aquilaria agallocha*
Family:	*Thymelaeaceae*
Distribution:	North India, Cambodia, Indonesia
Plant part:	wood
Scent:	woody, spicy, complex, multilayered, enticing
Uses:	rheumatism, asthma, gout, diarrhea; prayer, meditation, rituals
Properties:	stimulating, invigorating, relaxing, emotionally stabilizing, cleanses the soul

Eastern • precious • traditional

This precious incense wood, also known as *ud*, *oud*, gaharu wood, aloeswood, or eaglewood, is formed when the wood of the agar tree is infected by a fungal culture that stimulates the production of a special resin. In the wild, this can take up to a hundred years, but the incense available nowadays comes from sustainably grown plantations where the process has been reduced between five and fifteen years.

The incense has been documented as *ud* or *oud* (Arabic for wood) in India, Egypt, Israel, and the Arab world since ancient times, being first recorded in ancient Indian Sanskrit texts around 1700 BCE. The inhabitants of the Southeast Asian island of Borneo burn it as incense in traditional spirit-summoning rituals, while it is used in Islam on major feast days, and has been imported into Japan since the 7th century. Today it is one of the most valuable raw materials used in the perfume industry.

For use in smudging, agarwood is sold crushed into small pieces or as spills. Depending on the species, maturity, and quality of the wood, it can develop completely different fragrances.

Amber

Name:	*Succinite*
Family:	various deciduous and coniferous trees
Distribution:	global
Plant part:	fossil resin
Scent:	powerful, bitter, spicy, a little like myrrh, depending on the tree from which it comes
Uses:	protection and healing
Properties:	powerfully cleansing, warming, strengthening body and soul, relaxing

Tertiary period • known as a gemstone • used since the Neolithic period • a lengthy burning time

Amber is fossil resin from various deciduous and coniferous trees from the Tertiary period (which followed the end of the Cretaceous period approximately 65 million years ago and lasted for around 63 million years) and is found all over the world. In Europe the most famous amber, known as "northern gold," comes from the Baltic Sea area, but amber is also known to many cultures and has been widely used as a healing agent, such as in an oil to ease the pain of rheumatism. Amber was also used in many temple incense-burning rituals.

As amber burns for a long time, produces large amounts of smoke, and has a strong odor, it is particularly suitable as an ingredient in smudging blends, but it is less ideal used as a single ingredient. It works well in combination with benzoin.

Did you know? The descendants of many of the trees that produced the fossilized tree resin known as amber are still with us today. This is why the properties and scent of amber resemble those of the resins of other trees (Scots pine, spruce, juniper, fir, cedar, cypress, copal, mastic, styrax).

Angelica

Name:	*Angelica archangelica*
Family:	*Apiaceae* (umbellifers)
Distribution:	Northern & Central Europe
Plant part:	seeds, root, blossom
Scent:	aromatic, warm, earthy
Uses:	end-of-life care; cleansing and protection
Properties:	harmonious, protective, cleansing, antidepressant, transformative, grounding, enlightening, strengthens links with ancestors, aura-cleansing

wild plant • traditional • risk of confusion with poisonous hemlock or giant hogweed

Angelica originated in the Middle East but spread to the rest of continental Europe with the invasion of the Romans, although it did not reach the British Isles until the Middle Ages. Angelica is considered to have strong protective properties and in the medieval period was traditionally used to drive away ghosts and demons and offer protection against sorcery. According to legend, it acquired its name when the Archangel Michael appeared to a monk in a dream and recommended angelica as protection against the plague. Angelica was also used together with dragon's blood in exorcism rituals. When burned as incense, the smoke strengthens both the immune system and the mind, dispelling any negative energies that may be present in a room or are clinging to a person or object. It brings light on every level.

Many of us are familiar with the candied angelica root and stems used in food and to decorate cakes, and the plant is also popular as a herbal liqueur.

Aniseed/ Star Anise

Name:	*Pimpinella anisum/Illicium verum*
Family:	*Apiaceae* (umbellifers)/*Schisandraceae*
Distribution:	Eastern Mediterranean, West Asia/China, Vietnam
Plant part:	seeds
Scent:	fresh, spicy, fruity, sweet
Uses:	for balance, inner peace
Properties:	warming, relaxing, calming, mood-enhancing

Mediterranean and Asian spice • used in smudging blends

Despite their similar sounding names, aniseed and star anise are not related, although their seeds are similar in terms of their properties and so can be used interchangeably. Star anise is popular as a spice in Asian cooking and aniseed is used to flavor various alcoholic drinks and some baked goods. Aniseed is also often combined with caraway in teas to encourage lactation in breastfeeding mothers. It also has digestive and anticonvulsant properties and can help to relieve flatulence. Used in incense, both aniseed and star anise bring a touch of lightness to strong, heavy fragrances.

Did you know? The Japanese star anise tree or shrub (*Illicium anisatum*) bears similar fruit to genuine star anise and so the two are often confused. Be very careful, however, as the fruit of the Japanese star anise is poisonous!

Ash

Name:	*Fraxinus excelsior*
Family:	*Oleaceae*
Distribution:	Northern & Central Europe
Plant part:	seeds, leaves
Scent:	little scent of its own, smoky
Uses:	rheumatism, gout, fractures; transformation, divination, glimpses into past lives, willpower, focus, courage, self-confidence, self-worth, protection
Properties:	protective, cleansing

common • used in blends • Celtic-Germanic herbs and resins

The ash tree is closely associated with humans in many Indo-Germanic myths: in the Old Norse *Edda* cycle of narrative poems, the world tree Yggdrasil is assumed to be an ash tree, and Ask, the first human male in Norse mythology, is derived from *askr*, Old Norse for ash tree. A tree that likes to grow in moist soils, in alluvial forests, and along rivers and streams, the ash has a healing and calming effect on feelings and emotions.

Its use in herbal remedies is documented as long ago as the ancient world and products derived from ash trees are still used in medicine today: infusions made with the bark are used to treat stiffness in the muscles and joints and gout in particular, the ground bark helps to accelerate bone healing, and a tea made from the leaves or seeds is said to have diuretic properties.

Bay Leaf

Name:	*Laurus nobilis*
Family:	*Lauraceae* (laurel family)
Distribution:	Mediterranean region
Plant part:	leaves
Scent:	warm, mildly spicy, herbaceous, aromatic
Uses:	dreams, dedication, clairvoyance, invocations, the nights of Yuletide, visions; concentration, self-confidence, inner security, self-knowledge, cleansing, strength, success
Properties:	antiseptic, disinfectant, calming, opens the third eye

culinary herb • traditionally used in Southern Europe • popular in Greece and Rome since ancient times

Bay leaves come from the sweet bay tree, which has been cultivated since ancient times in the Mediterranean region. In Greece bay leaves were considered a panacea for all ills and were planted around temples in honor of the god Apollo. Pythia, the high priestess known as the famous Oracle of Delphi, would burn bay leaves together with henbane to clear her mind and open her third eye in order to receive visions.

Bay leaves were burned as incense in the Alpine region of Europe at the feast of Epiphany on January 6 to drive away the last spirits from the nights of Yuletide and to invite the power of the sun into the home for the coming year. Bay leaves should be burned in smudging in small quantities and/or in blends.

Benzoin

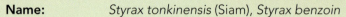

Name:	*Styrax tonkinensis* (Siam), *Styrax benzoin* (Sumatra)
Family:	*Styracaceae*
Distribution:	Southeast Asia, Borneo, Sumatra, Java
Plant part:	resin
Scent:	soothing, resinous, vanilla, warm
Uses:	depression, respiratory complaints; sorrow, (transition) rituals, inspiration and creativity
Properties:	antimicrobial, antiseptic, expectorant, anti-inflammatory, harmonious, sensual, comforting, warming, balancing, relaxing, warms the soul

popular as incense • from Indonesia • temple incense • often faked

The term benzoin applies to two kinds of resin: benzoin Sumatra, from Indochina, and benzoin Siam, which is indigenous to Southeast Asia. Both varieties are harvested from a species of styrax tree and are similar in their fragrance and uses, although benzoin Sumatra is a little sweeter and more subtle than its more expensive cousin. Benzoin Siam is one of the most popular incenses in Southeast Asia, while benzoin Sumatra is preferred in India.

Almost all incense sticks and cones contain benzoin, as does the oil used in the Catholic church to administer the last rites. The resin is used as temple incense in India and is also burned during the puja, the ceremonial offering ritual of Hindus and Buddhists. Finally, it can be used in treatments for respiratory complaints and skin conditions.

Benzoin burns quickly and generates copious amounts of pungent smoke, so it is more suitable for use in smudging blends than as a single ingredient. This versatile resin is often faked or cut with impurities, which can be detected by a slight odor of turpentine.

Birch

Name:	*Betula pendula* (silver birch), *Betula alba* (European white birch)
Family:	Betulaceae
Distribution:	Central & Eastern Europe, North America
Plant part:	leaves, bark, buds, wood
Scent:	fresh, woody (leaves, bark, wood); sweet, floral (buds)
Uses:	headaches, women's issues; new beginnings, at Candlemas, annual festivals, transition rituals, initiation, for self-confidence, creativity
Properties:	promotes concentration, enlightening

domestic/native tree • foraging plant • sacred to the Celtic and Germanic tribes

The birch tree has been part of our lives since the dawn of human history, with a long tradition of being used for practical, medicinal, and magical purposes. Each part of the tree can be put to good use, from its wood and bark for building boats and as a medium on which to write, to its resin (birch pitch), which was used as a caulking material and as chewing gum. Tinder fungus, which grows on the dead trunks of the birch, was used for lighting fires, and the sap that the trees produce in spring has recently been rediscovered in the form of refreshing, revitalizing birch water. Infused in a tea, the leaves have diuretic properties. The birch is associated with the month of May; it is a tree of light, new beginnings, and vitality, and the trunk was traditionally used to form the maypole. Witches' broomsticks were also said to be made from the brushwood of the birch.

Calamus

Name:	*Acorus Americanus*
Family:	*Acoraceae*
Distribution:	originally in Asia, now widespread
Plant part:	root
Scent:	bitter, aromatic, powerful
Uses:	combat stress, concentration, protection, success, self-confidence, energy
Properties:	bolstering the nerves, calming, balancing, energizing, powerfully reassuring

in smudging blends • Eastern • mentioned in the Bible • mildly toxic in high doses

Calamus has been a popular part of traditional Chinese medicine for many thousands of years, chiefly to aid digestion. Precisely when the use of calamus became more widespread is unknown, but it is known to have been an ingredient of the traditional *kyphi* incense balls of ancient Egypt, as well has having been used in offerings to the gods of Mesopotamia and as a tobacco substitute by the indigenous peoples of North America. In Ayurvedic medicine, calamus is used to treat shock and as an aphrodisiac, while the Christian Bible records its use both as an incense and as an ingredient in holy anointing oil. When intended for smudging, the root should be finely chopped, grated, or ground to a powder. Due to its pungent odor, calamus is rarely used as incense on its own but is burned in blends. It should also be used only in smaller quantities, as large doses can be toxic.

Camphor

Name:	*Cinnamomum camphora*
Family:	*Lauraceae* (laurel family)
Distribution:	China, Japan, Taiwan
Plant part:	distillate of plant parts
Scent:	powerful, spicy, hot, minty
Uses:	rheumatism, colds, as an insect repellent
Properties:	anticonvulsant, fortifies the nerves, cheering, stabilizing, powerfully cleansing, clarifying

traditionally used in Asia • to be burned as incense only in its natural form • an ingredient of tiger balm

Camphor is steam-distilled as an essential oil, mainly from the bark and wood of the camphor tree *Cinnamomum camphora*, and is popular in both Asia and the West as an ointment to rub on the chest to treat colds and flu, for back pain (in tiger balm), and rheumatism. In China it was used to treat headaches and in Ayurvedic medicine to calm the nerves due to its cooling properties. It was most commonly used as incense in South India, in pujas (especially in honor of Shiva) and for meditation. In the Arab world, on the other hand, the smoke was used to dampen romantic desire.

These days the camphor available for sale is mainly synthetic, but this form of camphor should not be used in smudging; be sure to use natural camphor only (derived from the camphor laurel). Camphor (whether synthetic or natural) should not be taken internally.

The camphor tree is grown as an ornamental tree in parts of North America.

Cardamom

Name:	*Elettaria cardamomum*
Family:	*Zingiberaceae*
Distribution:	South India, Guatemala, Tanzania
Plant part:	seeds
Scent:	pleasant, exotic, fresh
Uses:	love, self-confidence, courage, partnership, determination; insect repellent
Properties:	strengthens the nerves, aphrodisiac, harmonious, stimulates energy flow, antiseptic, disinfectant

a spice • Eastern

Green (or true) cardamom originates from South India, Thailand, and Iraq but is now mainly cultivated in Guatemala and Tanzania. We are generally primarily aware of cardamom seeds as a spice ingredient in North African and Asian dishes, but as a medicinal plant it boosts the stomach and nerves and is effective against flatulence. However, cardamom was already being used as incense by the ancient Egyptians. The seeds are prepared by crushing or grinding them to a powder, but only just before a smudging ritual is ready to start, as their volatile substances evaporate quickly.

Cedar

Name:	*Cedrus atlantica* (Atlas cedar), *Cedrus brevifolia* (Cyprus cedar), *Cedrus libani* (cedar of Lebanon), *Cedrus deodara* (Himalayan cedar)
Family:	Pinaceae
Distribution:	North Africa, Eastern Mediterranean, Himalayas
Plant part:	wood, resin, needles, bark
Scent:	warm, perfumed, spicy
Uses:	anxiety and stress, sacrificial offerings, prayer, dreams, new beginnings, courage, cleansing, healing
Properties:	healing, relaxing, invigorating, harmonious

Eastern • sacred tree

The four species of cedar named above are often confused in textbooks with the North American cedar, see Cedar (American), opposite page. The latter is actually a species of juniper and therefore belongs to the cypress family. The difference is obvious, at least as far as the needles and shoot tips are concerned: true cedars have short, smooth, spiky needles similar to those of their relation the Scots pine, while the needles of the American cedar are delicate, with small overlapping scales similar to the foliage of the thuja, to which it is related.

True cedars were sacred for many ancient peoples, and its fragrant, durable wood was used for building everything from chests and sarcophagi to houses and ships. The resin in particular was used medicinally and as incense—the words for frankincense and cedar were interchangeable in the language of ancient Mesopotamia. Cedar of Lebanon was in such high demand that the great forests were felled and now just a few small forests remain.

Cedar (American)

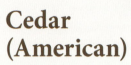

Name:	*Juniperus* spp., *Thuja* spp.
Family:	*Cupressaceae*
Distribution:	North America
Plant part:	tips of the shoots, needles
Scent:	green, resinous, spicy
Uses:	respiratory conditions; (sweat lodge) rituals, healing, cleansing, clarity, opening the self
Properties:	cleansing, protection from negative energies

traditionally used in North America • sacred tree of Native Americans • sweat lodge

Contrary to what the name might suggest, American cedars are not related to the true cedars of the *Pinaceae* family but are a species of juniper which, much like the common juniper that grows throughout the northern hemisphere, are among the oldest and most important incense and medicinal plants. This type of cedar is considered sacred by the Native Americans, who used to (and still do) burn the tips of its shoots as incense in important rituals due to its ability to carry prayers and songs to the gods. The tips of the shoots were also burned with white sage and fragrant sweetgrass (also known as Mary's grass) during sweat lodge rituals, which mostly served ceremonial purposes in addition to their physical hygiene and social uses. Cedar twigs could also be found in the medicine bags of the indigenous peoples of North and Central America.

Chamomile

- **Name:**
- **Family:** *Asteraceae* (daisy family)
- **Distribution:** global
- **Plant part:** flowers, leaves
- **Scent:** soothing, soft, sweet, herbaceous
- **Uses:** gastrointestinal complaints, stress, fear, insomnia; meditation, summer solstice, healing and harmony, as a sun herb
- **Properties:** anti-inflammatory, calming, relaxing

domestic wild plant • one of the oldest known medicinal plants • well-known and popular

Chamomile's popularity as a medicinal plant dates as far back as the Neolithic era. Taken internally as a tea, it is mainly drunk to treat stomach pain, gastrointestinal complaints, colds, and infections, but can also be applied to wounds to accelerate healing and as a topical treatment for skin inflammation. Chamomile also calms the mind and so helps to promote sleep. Related to feverfew, it can help to ease pelvic complaints when added to a bath.

Cinnamon

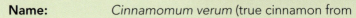

Name:	*Cinnamomum verum* (true cinnamon from Sri Lanka), *Cinnamomum cassia* (Chinese cassia)
Family:	*Lauraceae* (laurel family)
Distribution:	India, China, Malaysia, Japan, Vietnam, parts of South America and Africa
Plant part:	bark, flowers
Scent:	heavy, sweet, warm, soft, aromatic
Uses:	fear, anxiety, men's issues, concentration
Properties:	warming, aphrodisiac, harmonious, brings good energies, sensual

a spice • Eastern

The cinnamon we use today is sourced from two different trees and is sold as true cinnamon, the original spice, and Chinese cassia (Chinese cinnamon). Both kinds are made from dried bark and have a similar scent and properties when used in smudging. Cinnamon first became popular in the Arab world before spreading to Greece, Rome, and North Africa. Cinnamon oil was used for embalming in Egypt because of its preservative and antiseptic properties, while cassia was a popular smudging ingredient and formed part of the anointing oil described in the Christian Bible. The Western world uses cinnamon and cloves in Christmas spice blends.

Cloves

Name:	*Syzygium aromaticum*
Family:	*Myrtaceae*
Distribution:	India and around the Indian Ocean
Plant part:	dried flower buds
Scent:	warm, spicy
Uses:	concentration, intuition, creativity, happiness, love, letting go, self-worth; insect repellent
Properties:	aphrodisiac, harmonious, inspiring, disinfectant, aura-cleansing

a spice • used for dental pain relief

Cloves do not grow in Western climates but originally came from the Maluku Islands (also known as the Moluccas or Spice Islands) and the Southern Philippines. Oil of cloves has a long history of use in Chinese and Ayurvedic medicine for toothache. As an incense, cloves are used to drive away evil spirits and are a common ingredient of Indian, Japanese, and Tibetan incense sticks.

Copal

Name:	*Bursera* spp., *Protium* spp.
Family:	Burseraceae
Distribution:	Central and South America, the Caribbean, parts of Africa
Plant part:	resin
Scent:	delicate, lemony, woody, light (white); soft, warm, resinous (golden); mystical, fragrant, heavy, earthy (black)

white

Uses:	blessings, rituals, initiation, divination, mental and spiritual work
Properties:	refreshing, cleansing, healing, opens the individual up to the divine

golden

Uses:	in morning smudging sessions, for intuition, creativity, protection
Properties:	clarifying, reassuring, mood-enhancing, opens up the senses

black

Uses:	in life crises, contacting ancestors
Properties:	calming, touches the soul

traditionally used in Central and South America • various amber-like resins • from trees from a range of different plant families

Resins from various trees are sold as copal, including Australian copal from the kauri tree (*Agathis australis*), East Indian copal from *Canarium bengalense*, and Manila copal from the dammar pine (*Agathis dammara guma*). However, the authentic copal comes from the *Myroxylon* genus of Central America, where it has been burned as incense since the arrival of Columbus in sacrifice to the gods and as an important part of initiation and divination rituals. It was sacred for the people of the Maya civilisation. There are three varieties that differ in color and scent: white and black copal were placed with the dead to provide sustenance in the afterlife and were used to make contact with tribal ancestors. Golden opal was burned in honor of the sunrise.

Cypress

Name:	*Cupressus sempervirens*
Family:	*Cupressaceae*
Distribution:	Mediterranean region, Asia
Plant part:	tips of the shoots, wood
Scent:	fresh, green, soft
Uses:	respiratory complaints; sorrow, transition rituals, parting, dedication, protection, blessings
Properties:	grounding, focusing, concentration, uplifting

well-known Mediterranean tree • used since ancient times

In the ancient world the cypress tree was a symbol and attribute of a number of different divinities. It was associated with long life, but also with death and mourning and the connection between the living and the dead, and so was planted as a symbol of sorrow. According to Hildegard von Bingen, the cypress provides protection against the devil, and its twigs were certainly burned to ward off demons and evil spirits. Cypress oil is now used in natural healing to treat many ailments and disorders, including colds and muscle and joint pain, while small cypress twigs are ideal for making smudge sticks.

Dammar Gum

Name:	*Canarium strictum, Canarium prostratum; Shorea wieseneri,* among others
Family:	*Burseraceae; Dipterocarpaceae*
Distribution:	India, Southeast Asia
Plant part:	resin
Scent:	dark dammar gum: spicy, aromatic, warm white dammar gum: lemony, fresh, fruity
Uses:	sorrow, depression, melancholy; light-bringer, contact with angels (white dammar gum)
Properties:	enlightening, balancing, clarifying, cleansing, protective

Eastern • can be an alternative to frankincense • known in the West as "cat's eye resin"

As is often the case with resins used as incense, the resin from various trees of Southeast Asian origin are all described as dammar gum. The main source is the *Shorea wieseneri* tree. Black dammar gum (*Canarium strictum*) is from the *Burseraceae* family, while white dammar gum is from the *Hopea, Shorea,* and *Vateria* genera of the *Dipterocarpaceae* family from India. Each variety has different scents and properties. Dammar gum is well suited for using as a sole ingredient in smudging, although when warmed over a heat source it should be placed on a bed of sand as the resin will liquefy.

Dragon's Blood

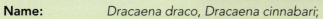

Name:	*Dracaena draco, Dracaena cinnabari; Daemonorops draco; Croton draco*
Family:	*Palmae, Arecaceae; Agavoideae; Euphorbiaceae*
Distribution:	Canary Islands, Madeira, Cape Verde; Southeast Asia, Java, Borneo, Maluku Islands; Central America
Plant part:	resin
Scent:	dark, warm, sweet
Uses:	blessings, rituals, exorcisms; protection, cleansing, love, fertility
Properties:	cleansing, invigorating, liberating

Asian-Indonesian • sourced from various plants • traditionally used in rituals

As with a number of other herbs and resins, the common name dragon's blood covers various incense substances from a wide range of plant families. One such comes from the Canary Islands dragon tree (an agave) whose resin is used medicinally, while another (related) example is the cinnabari dragon tree from the island of Socotra (Yemen). Both species are deep crimson in color, which gives the resin its name. A further type of dragon's blood comes from Central America and is obtained from the red sap of a member of the spurge family. It was once offered in sacrifices in place of real blood. The *Calamus draco* from Asia, a rattan plant whose flowers and fruit secrete a resin that was once popular as a dye but is now little used, is not related to the dragon's blood tree.

All varieties serve very well as binding agents for oils and resins, and can enhance the properties of other incense substances. Dragon's blood has potent protective properties and its cleansing smoke is said to be able to reset all energies to zero, which is why it has a long history of use in exorcism rituals. After a smudging session involving dragon's blood sourced from *Daemonorops draco*, it is important to build up positive energy—dragon's blood from *Dracaena cinnabari*, although difficult to find, is an excellent basis for this.

Elder

Name:	*Sambucus nigra*
Family:	*Adoxaceae*
Distribution:	Europe, parts of North & South America
Plant part:	bark, flowers, berries, wood, heartwood
Scent:	spicy, earthy, bitter, woody (wood and bark); smooth, sweet, honeyed (flowers); bitter, fruity (berries)
Uses:	taking leave of someone or something, sorrow, the nights of Yuletide, dreams, transition; protection
Properties:	blessings, healing, strengthening links with ancestors

small domestic tree • foraging plant • ancient plant used for protection, healing, and magic • Alpine shamanism • toxic (apart from the flowers and cooked berries; the berries must not be consumed raw)

Elder trees are found across Europe and have been used in herbal medicine and for magical purposes since prehistoric times. Many myths and superstitions have grown up around the elder. It is said to be possessed by a benevolent familiar spirit and so can bring good luck to a house or home, but felling an elder will bring misfortune and invoke the wrath of the fairy folk; cradles should not be made of its wood or the child will be pinched black and blue or might even be kidnapped by the fairies. Elder is also considered a "threshold tree" that can provide links to our ancestors.

Of all its many medicinal uses, the tea made with its flowers is best known for helping to reduce fever caused by infection. It reduces phlegm, opens the chest, and promotes perspiration while also acting as a mild sedative that can help to promote sleep. Elder leaves can be used to treat skin inflammation, and the berries can be cooked to make a juice or syrup that boosts the immune system and supports the formation of blood. It is generally the heartwood and flowers that are used for smudging, as all the other parts of the tree are toxic. The flowers are delicate and so are preferably heated over a teapot warmer.

Elecampane

Name:	*Inula helenium*
Family:	*Asteraceae* (daisy family)
Distribution:	Central Asia, Europe, Japan, North America
Plant part:	root
Scent:	gentle, mild, pleasant
Uses:	respiratory conditions, concentration; blessings, cleansing, summer solstice, self-confidence, protection
Properties:	memory-boosting, reassuring, protective, cleansing, antiseptic, antidepressant, cheering, warming

domestic • commonplace medicinal plant • traditionally used in Northern and Central Europe

Elecampane is a traditional component of herb bundles. It is the dried root of this ancient medicinal plant that is used in smudging, with the smoke said to have the power to cast out demons. It is used to bless amulets and ritual objects and to promote clairvoyance, especially in respect of nature spirits. Taken as a tea or wine, it loosens phlegm, strengthens the lungs, and soothes a cough. The root has powerful antibacterial properties, which is why it was once used to sterilize or as a poultice for wounds that were ulcerating or healing poorly.

Elemi

Name:	*Canarium luzonicum*
Family:	*Burseraceae*
Distribution:	Philippines
Plant part:	resin
Scent:	soft, clear, lemony, woody
Uses:	meditation, morning smudging session, concentration, inspiration, clairvoyance
Properties:	clarifying, refreshing, cleansing, energizing, mood-enhancing, sharpens the senses

for cleansing blends • an Asian resin

As with guggul (the resin of *Commiphora mukul*, the mukul myrrh tree indigenous to India), a number of different resins are described by the umbrella term elemi. One example is incense from *Boswellia frereana*, known as African elemi, although the elemi sourced from *Canarium luzonicum* (also from the *Burseraceae* family) is also sold as copal. The elemi tree is now principally cultivated in the Philippines where it is native. Its viscous resin, though difficult to work with, is used mainly in smudging blends as it harmonizes well with other herbs and resins that have cleansing properties.

Eucalyptus

Name:	*Eucalyptus* spp.
Family:	*Myrtaceae*
Distribution:	Australia, parts of North America
Plant part:	leaves, wood, and fruit
Scent:	fresh, pleasant, aromatic, camphoraceous, herbaceous
Uses:	concentration, harmony, energy; insect repellent
Properties:	invigorating, reassuring, revitalizing, stimulating, refreshing, cleansing, antiseptic

traditionally used in Australia • an effective medicinal plant with many uses • particularly used in treatments for the common cold

More than six hundred varieties of this tree are known. It is native to Australia, where the indigenous people would use it to combat infectious disease. We now use eucalyptus (often in combination with mint) in a range of cold remedies, but it can also be used to treat inflammatory conditions of the gastrointestinal tract. As an incense ingredient in smudging, the smoke generated from the eucalyptus cleanses the air in a room, driving away evil spirits and pathogens, and boosting our powers of concentration.

Frankincense

Name:	*Boswellia carteri/sacra* (olibanum), *Boswellia papyrifera*, *Boswellia serrata* (guggul), *Boswellia frereana* (elemi)
Family:	Burseraceae
Distribution:	Arabian Peninsula, North and Northeast Africa, India
Plant part:	resin
Scent:	delicate, warm, sweet, soothing
Uses:	toothache, fever, inflammation, psoriasis, polyarthritis, rheumatism, asthma, circulatory complaints, muscle tension; prayer, meditation, spirituality, cleansing, healing, clarity
Properties:	analgesic, cooling, disinfectant, wound-healing, calming, relaxing

in use since ancient times • a traditional incense of the Roman Catholic and Orthodox churches • Eastern • a wide variation in quality • look out for ethical sources

Frankincense is one of the most refined resins burned as incense and is mentioned in the Christian Bible as among the gifts brought by the three wise men. It is sourced from various species of the frankincense tree (*Boswellia* spp.), with the best frankincense coming from Oman (recognizable by its bright, clear, yellow coloration). Other classic varieties come from the south of the Arabian Peninsula, Northeast Africa, and the Middle East. Poorer quality frankincense can be identified by its very dark color and may also contain small pieces of bark. Incisions are made in the bark of the tree and the droplets of pitch that are exuded are collected once they have dried.

Frankincense has been one of the key resins used for sacred purposes since ancient times and was exported across the world from an early date. It is most familiar to the Western world from Catholic church services. The antimicrobial and cleansing properties of frankincense were soon noted, along with the relief that it brings to inflammation and pain, with the medicinal effects of Indian frankincense (*Boswellia serrata/guggul*) in particular having been proven in studies. The smoke of frankincense can be used to bathe the entire body in smudging rituals, p. 42.

Galangal

Name:	*Alpinia officinarum*
Family:	*Zingiberaceae*
Distribution:	East Asia, Himalayas
Plant part:	root
Scent:	light, hot, spicy, peppery
Uses:	gastrointestinal complaints, colds, fever
Properties:	invigorating, revitalizing, stimulating, warming, anti-inflammatory, expectorant

related to turmeric and ginger • herbal remedy • an Asian spice

In ancient times galangal was traded across the world, being exported from the Himalayas, where it originates, to Egypt, Mesopotamia, Greece, and Rome. It was used as a remedy for gastrointestinal complaints and digestive problems in much the same way as its close relative ginger. Galangal helps to fight colds and strengthens the immune system—for Benedictine abbess and polymath Hildegard of Bingen, it was the spice of life. Galangal is an ingredient of the German herbal remedy Klosterfrau Melissengeist (similar to Carmelite Water), that is made with 13 medicinal plants and is used as a household remedy for a host of complaints. Also known as Thai ginger and Siamese ginger, galangal is used in traditional Chinese medicine to promote digestion and treat conditions of the digestive system. In India and Tibet, galangal is principally known as an incense ingredient.

Galbanum

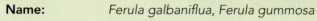

Name:	*Ferula galbaniflua, Ferula gummosa*
Family:	*Apiaceae, Umbelliferae*
Distribution:	Iran, Lebanon
Plant part:	resin
Scent:	green, mossy, resinous, woody
Uses:	tension, anxiety, women's issues (see below); protection, cleansing, shamanism
Properties:	calming, relaxing, grounding, promotes menstruation

mentioned in the Bible • Eastern • "mother resin"

Galbanum, also known as "mother resin," is one of the oldest traditional incense substances and is mentioned in the Bible alongside myrrh and frankincense. It is traditionally used to drive away negative energies ("evil spirits") and so is a popular choice for smudging blends intended to protect or cleanse. Its cleansing properties act on a fundamental level and can help to soften and dissolve entrenched beliefs and mental blockages. The ancient Greeks used the smoke to treat women's issues, to encourage menstruation, and as an abortifacient. Galbanum should therefore be avoided during pregnancy in order to help reduce the risk of miscarriage. The resin tends to be viscous and sticky. Warming it slightly (in a glass container) in a bain-marie or bowl of warm water will help to counteract this.

Guggul

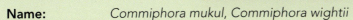

Name:	*Commiphora mukul, Commiphora wightii*
Family:	*Burseraceae*
Distribution:	India, Pakistan
Plant part:	resin
Scent:	bitter, resinous, perfumed
Uses:	joint complaints, respiratory conditions, stress, rheumatism, insomnia, mental stability; rituals, evening smudging sessions, healing, harmony, partnership, love, cleansing
Properties:	antiseptic, disinfectant, anti-inflammatory, analgesic, tissue-cleansing, invigorating, strengthening the body's defenses, balancing, aphrodisiac, detoxifying

traditionally used in Ayurvedic medicine • Arabic burnt offering/Asian incense • popular as incense

Guggul is a gum resin traditionally extracted from the trunk of myrrh or other trees of the *Commiphora* genus. It has a range of uses in Ayurvedic medicine, including detoxifying the nervous system, strengthening the uterus, and alleviating skin conditions, as well as treating a range of urological and neurological diseases. The smoke can be inhaled to treat colds and reduce inflammation, but guggul is also used for magical and spiritual purposes, and in the Arab world is burned as an offering in much the same way as frankincense.

Did you know? Known in Hindi as *guggulu*, meaning "that which protects from disease," the resin of *Commiphora* spp., the guggul tree, is known as Indian myrrh or Indian bdellium. The bdellium cited in ancient texts is no longer sold officially, as it is hard to be sure from which plant it has been sourced (presumably *Commiphora africana*). Indian frankincense from *Boswellia serrata* is also sold as guggul, so always check before making a purchase.

Hops

Name:	*Humulus lupulus*
Family:	*Cannabaceae*
Distribution:	Europe, North America
Plant part:	cones (flowers consisting of layers of petals), young leaves, glands of the female flowers (lupulin)
Scent:	bitter, aromatic, hoppy
Uses:	muscle tension, insomnia; dreams, new beginnings, nights of Yuletide, harmony and balance
Properties:	calming, relaxing

traditionally used in Europe • associated with the brewing of beer

Hops were originally native to Southern Europe, from where they spread northward. Today hops are rarely found growing in the wild but are widely cultivated for the brewing of beer. It is the glands of the cone-like flowers of the female plant that are generally used in herbal medicine and smudging. The calming effect of hops is well known, but they can also intensify feelings of sadness in those who are depressed and so should be avoided in such circumstances (the same applies for drinking beer rich in hops). Less well known is the fact that the female flowers contain phytoestrogens that can help with menopause-related complaints.

When hops are used as incense, it is preferable to burn them on an incense burner with a mesh rather than on charcoal. This applies whether using them on their own in small quantities or in blends. Hops are also useful as an ingredient in a sleep-promoting smudging session in the evening.

Hyssop

Name:	*Hyssopus officinalis*
Family:	*Lamiaceae*
Distribution:	Europe, parts of Africa
Plant part:	green parts, leaves, blossom
Scent:	warm, spicy
Uses:	respiratory complaints, depression, concentration; blessings, joy in life, cleansing (including ritual objects)
Properties:	antiseptic, disinfectant, invigorating, bracing

- traditionally used in medicine and rituals since the Middle Ages
- "pleasant-smelling herb"

Hyssop was first described by the ancient Greeks (the hyssop mentioned in the Christian Bible is almost certainly another plant), but its name derives from the Hebrew *ezob*, meaning "pleasant-smelling herb." It was originally indigenous to the Mediterranean region but found its way across large parts of Europe with the Romans, and was one of the herbs strewn on medieval floors to keep away the plague (and witches).

Hyssop is traditionally used to treat bronchial disorders, in particular to loosen the phlegm that accompanies a cough. When taken as a tea, it can be effective against parasitic worms and aid digestion, and when applied as an ointment, it helps to soothe rheumatoid arthritis and to heal superficial skin injuries. Hildegard of Bingen, the 12th-century abbess and mystic, recommended it as a treatment for coughs and depression. The smoke generated by hyssop in smudging is particularly cleansing and protective for people, spaces, and ritual objects. It boosts and invigorates the body and mind, sharpens the wits, and promotes concentration.

Iris

Name:	*Iris germanica, Iris cretica*
Family:	*Iridaceae*
Distribution:	Europe
Plant part:	root
Scent:	soft, warm, mild
Uses:	emotional blockages, grief and sorrow, end-of-life care, transition rituals; love, spiritual awakening
Properties:	inspiring, liberating, soothes pain

rarely found in the wild • garden plant

The root of the iris should be stored for several years to allow it to develop its typical light scent reminiscent of violets. Children with teething problems are still sometimes given dried iris root (known as orris root) to chew (not recommended because of possible toxicity if ingested and the risk of choking). In powdered form, iris root is mainly used as a carrier substance for essential oils. When burned on its own in smudging, iris helps to break down emotional blockages and heal old wounds. It also helps with letting go, especially in end-of-life care, where it supports both the dying and their friends and relatives.

Juniper

Name:	*Juniperus communis*
Family:	*Cupressaceae*
Distribution:	Eurasia, North America
Plant part:	berries, twigs, wood, resin
Scent:	warm, pleasant, resinous
Uses:	rheumatism, colds and flu, convalescence, concentration; annual festivals, nights of Yuletide, Christmas, visions, divination, bad dreams, transition rituals, parting; protection, cleansing
Properties:	strengthens links with ancestors, cleansing, revitalizing, antiseptic, destroys germs

protected domestic tree/shrub • prehistoric • spice • risk of confusion with the highly poisonous savin juniper (*Juniperus sabina*) • see also Cedar (p. 113).

Species of juniper have been used in smudging and for medicinal purposes wherever it is found growing. Common juniper is one of the oldest plants known to have been used as incense in the home and in the shelters of livestock, and is recorded on an ancient Egyptian papyrus some 4,000 years old. The blue-black berries of the European species are traditionally not only used as a spice (and to flavor alcohol) but also to treat everything from gastrointestinal complaints to rheumatism.

Juniper may no longer be used to protect against the plague, but it is still put to good use in fighting colds and flu. Juniper resin has a long history of use as a substitute for frankincense. Common juniper is a protected species when growing in the wild, but bushes are often cultivated in gardens and the berries can be found in any supermarket.

Did you know? The incense commercially available as cedar or American cedar, particularly in Native American smudge sticks, is also sourced from species of juniper from the *Juniperus* and *Thuja* familes, and is only distantly related to true cedars (*Pinaceae*).

Labdanum

Name:	*Cistus ladanifer, Cistus creticus*
Family:	*Cistaceae*
Distribution:	Southwestern Mediterranean
Plant part:	resin
Scent:	complex and transient, herbaceous, vanilla
Uses:	depression, states of shock, sorrow, blockages; visions (the subconscious), meditation, love
Properties:	grounding, sensual, warming

rare and expensive • traditionally used in the Mediterranean • originates from rockrose, a familiar medicinal plant

Labdanum, also known as ladanum, is the sticky resin exuded by the rockrose. In centuries past it would be harvested by driving a herd of goats through the plants and then combing out the resin that had adhered to their coats, but today a special leather rake is used. Labdanum smoke was once used to help expel the placenta after birth. In Crete women would use it as a perfume, while elsewhere in Europe, smudging with labdanum was used to soothe toothache and as protection against the plague.

Labdanum is a viscous, sticky mass similar to galbanum and is difficult to separate into usable portions. In this case gentle warming may be helpful, or freezing into a block from which shavings can be grated. For smudging purposes, the dried foliage of the rockrose can be used as a substitute for labdanum. Although labdanum was popular and widespread in the ancient world, it has become less common and expensive.

Lady's Mantle

Name:	*Alchemilla vulgaris*
Family:	*Rosaceae*
Distribution:	Europe
Plant part:	upper parts and flowering stalks
Scent:	herbaceous, bitter, warm
Uses:	women's issues, love and fertility rituals; summer solstice, creativity, intuition
Properties:	grounding, protective, calming

common • foraging plant • familiar medicinal plant

Lady's mantle was originally native to Northern Europe, where it can still be found in the highest mountains ranges and as far north as the Arctic Circle, and later spread to the rest of Europe. The name hints at its traditional use as a medicinal plant for women's aliments: it regulates the menstrual cycle and hormonal imbalance in women, promotes contractions of the uterus, fights infection, and is said to stimulate the flow of milk (the root in particular contains phytohormones similar to progesterone). It also helps with the healing of wounds, while gargling or rinsing with the plant as a tea can be useful to treat inflammation of the mouth or throat.

The small drops of liquid seen on the leaves of Lady's mantle in the morning might at first appear to be dew, but they are in fact exuded by the plant itself. They were prized by medieval alchemists and credited with special healing powers. These droplets would be used by women to refresh the skin, invigorate its tissue, and smooth out wrinkles. Lady's mantle was also burned as incense in a love charm.

Larch

Name:	*Larix decidua*
Family:	*Pinaceae*
Distribution:	Europe
Plant part:	resin, cones, bark, needles, wood
Scent:	refined, powerful, perfumed, refreshing, woody
Uses:	depression, respiratory complaints, anxiety; insecurity, self-confidence, courage
Properties:	antiseptic, stimulates blood flow, anti-inflammatory, anticonvulsant, warming, cheering, relaxing, stimulating, bracing, motivating

deciduous conifer • traditionally used in folk medicine, for example in Alpine regions

The larch is the only deciduous conifer native to Europe, losing its needles in winter. Many tales and customs are associated with the larch, and its various parts have long been used in smudging rituals intended to bring good luck or bless a new beginning. Like most other resins from coniferous trees, larch resin can be used to treat respiratory complaints, especially stubborn mucus, and in the past the medicinal resin called Venice turpentine (known as such because it was traded through the port of Venice in Italy), also made from the larch, was used to stop bleeding and to treat earache, skin conditions, and other complaints. Larch turpentine (larch balm) can also be used as incense.

Lavender

Name:	*Lavandula angustifolia*
Family:	*Lamiaceae*
Distribution:	Europe, North America
Plant part:	flowers, leaves, entire plant
Scent:	refreshing, smooth, sweet
Uses:	insomnia, anxiety; harmony, protection, cleansing, inspiration, divination, intuition; insect repellent
Properties:	energizing, invigorating, calming, cleansing, clarifying, disinfectant, antispasmodic, antibacterial

Mediterranean wild plant • garden plant • well known and popular • traditionally used since ancient times

Lavandula angustifolia (common names include English lavender, though it is not native to England) originally grew wild in Southwestern Europe before making its way across much of the rest of the world with the Romans, eventually reaching North America with European settlers. The name derives from the Latin *lavare*, meaning "to wash." Lavender has been cultivated in Europe north of the Alps since the 8th century, but the largest fields and the best-quality plants are still to be found along the Mediterranean coast, where lavender has been extremely popular since ancient times. The Romans added it to bathwater and the ancient Greeks and Persians used lavender to fumigate sickrooms. It also repels mosquitoes, moths, and bacteria, not to mention energy vampires and negative vibrations.

Used to cleanse the air in children's rooms, lavender can help them to settle down at the end of a long day, blessing the children themselves in addition. However, recent studies have shown that lavender contains a phytoestrogen that can stimulate breast growth in prepubescent children, so caution should be exercised in the case of young children.

Lavender's effectiveness as a sleeping aid and a treatment for restlessness and nervous gastrointestinal conditions has been medically proven. As with hops, lavender is stimulating in small doses and relaxing in larger quantities. The flowers may pop and explode during smudging, causing scorch marks on carpets, furniture, and clothing, or even minor burns to the skin, so it is preferable to grind them to a powder.

Lemon Balm

Name:	*Melissa officinalis*
Family:	*Lamiaceae*
Distribution:	Europe, North & South America, Middle East
Plant part:	leaves
Scent:	lemon, spicy
Uses:	fear, insomnia, shock, stress, sorrow; evening smudging sessions, concentration, strength, joy, success; insect repellent
Properties:	calming, relaxing, harmonious, steels the nerves, mood-enhancing

domestic garden plant • culinary herb • foraging plant • bee pasture • component of herb bundles

Lemon balm has been used for medicinal purposes since ancient times and, as was the case with many other herbs from the Mediterranean region, we have the 8th-century Frankish king Charlemagne to thank for bringing it from its original home to the rest of Europe. Hildegard of Bingen, 12th-century abbess and mystic, recommended lemon balm as a cardiac tonic that would bring a cheerful heart and pleasant dreams. Carmelite nuns (members of the Order of the Brother of the Blessed Virgin Mary of Mount Carmel) developed Klosterfrau, a tonic of which lemon balm is the principal ingredient, to settle the nerves. Lemon balm also strengthens the gastrointestinal tract, helps against colds and fevers, and can be found in many herb bouquets. It is not generally used for smudging on its own, as its own scent is highly volatile and evaporates quickly, but it is an essential part of any calming smudging blends.

Marigold

Name:	*Calendula officinalis*
Family:	*Asteraceae* (daisy family)
Distribution:	Europe, India, China, Australia, parts of the Americas
Plant part:	flowers
Scent:	floral, gentle
Uses:	protection; light-bringer, sunflower
Properties:	mood-enhancing, warming, cheering, comforting, antiseptic, strengthens the heart

important medicinal plant • domestic garden plant • foraging plant • not commonly used as incense

The marigold or calendula is sunshine in flower form. Native to Spain, it now grows in much of the rest of the world. It is an important medicinal plant used to treat wounds, as its antiseptic properties help to keep open wounds germ-free and promote healing. Ointment made with marigold also helps to treat inflammation, burns, and bruising. When taken as a tea or in extract form, marigold helps to soothe fever and internal inflammation. The flowers of some types of marigold can be eaten (but not all are recommended for consumption). Marigold flowers should be burned on a mesh as they burn too quickly on charcoal.

Mastic

Name:	*Pistacia lentiscus*
Family:	*Anacardiaceae*
Distribution:	Mediterranean region
Plant part:	resin
Scent:	lemon, fresh, fruity
Uses:	invocation, dedication, meditation, intuition, visions; sense of security, happiness, spirituality, a balm for the soul, light-bringer; energy and strength
Properties:	enlivening, reassuring, magical, clarifying, cleansing

aromatic • used in smudging blends • popular in Greece

Most of the mastic used today comes from the Greek island of Chios in the Aegean Sea (it is also known as "tears of Chios"), and it is still used in Greece as a flavoring for baked goods, liqueurs, and wine. When mixed with white wax and other incense substances, it produces the wax-mastic that is used as an aromatic in the Greek Orthodox Church. As incense, it helps an individual to be receptive to visions and the world above, cleansing both body and soul. In incense blends, mastic intensifies the scents of the individual components and helps to combine them into a harmonious whole.

Meadowsweet (Mead Wort)

Name:	*Filipendula ulmaria*
Family:	*Rosaceae*
Distribution:	Europe/Eurasia, parts of North America
Plant part:	flowers, leaves
Scent:	vanilla, almond, sweet, warm, soft
Uses:	rheumatism, flu, stomach pain, women's issues; transition rituals, new beginnings, dreams, summer solstice, love, intuition, protection, letting go of the old, light-bringer
Properties:	calming, antiseptic, disinfectant, destroys germs, soothes pain

domestic wild plant • foraging plant • traditional medicinal plant

Meadowsweet was originally indigenous to the British Isles but subsequently spread to Southern Europe and elsewhere. It is one of the plants from which Blodeuwedd, a female figure in Welsh Celtic mythology, is said to have been made, and so is still associated with virginal goddesses and brides. Smudging with meadowsweet was used to treat disorders among livestock—especially those that produced milk, such as cows and goats—and the udders of the females would be washed in a decoction of the plant. It was also used for cleansing or disinfecting beehives. When used as herbal medicine for humans, meadowsweet helps to treat rheumatic complaints and influenza. It contains salicylic acid and gives its name to aspirin (via its former botanical name *Spiraea ulmaria*). Taken as a tea, the plant is extremely effective against all forms of stomach pain, while as a smudging ingredient, it drives away pathogens and the tendency to cling mentally to vestiges of the past, bringing light into our lives. When burned in smudging, it is preferable to place the delicate flowers on a mesh.

Mistletoe

Name:	*Viscum album*
Family:	*Santalaceae*
Distribution:	Eurasia, North Africa
Plant part:	all parts
Scent:	very little scent of its own
Uses:	high blood pressure, epilepsy; nights of Yuletide, divination, dreams, protection
Properties:	transformative, enlightening, opens the mind, anticonvulsant, calming, strengthens links with ancestors

wild plant • Celtic ritual plant • often found growing semi-parasitically on apple trees, poplars, hawthorn, and Scots pines • foraging plant • toxic

Species of the *Viscum* genus were found all over the ancient world. Today there are three subvarieties of white-berried mistletoe, differentiated by their host tree into deciduous, fir, and pine mistletoe. Mistletoe preparations may be able to help treat high blood pressure, epilepsy, and seizures, as well as to support tumor therapy.

Mistletoe was a sacred plant for the Celtic Druids. When being cut for rituals, great care was taken to ensure that the plant, which has no contact with the ground as it grows and is therefore a "heavenly" plant, was caught in a cloth, as it was believed to lose its power if it touched the ground. The Celts also believed that mistletoe could make a person invisible. When burned in smudging, its smoke opens up the subconscious and brings elements of dreams and the unconscious out into the light so that we can understand them. It transforms negative vibrations, including radiation, into positive, and supports the flow of energy. Growing as it does between heaven and earth, and remaining green and bearing fruit even in winter, mistletoe is symbolic, representing eternal life and rebirth. It can help us to connect with our ancestors.

Mistletoe should be used sparingly, as every part is toxic. It is more suitable for use in blends than for smudging on its own.

Did you know? As white mistletoe draws its nutrients from its host tree, it takes on that tree's energy and therefore also contains the essence of the host, which may be a consideration when smudging. Mistletoe grows very slowly and is rare on some trees. It should therefore be cut only from trees where it is commonly found and abundant—if a tree has a large quantity of mistletoe, it may even do it good to lose a little.

Mugwort

Name:	*Artemisia vulgaris*
Family:	*Asteraceae* (daisy family)
Distribution:	global
Plant part:	root, tips of the shoots, leaves
Scent:	earthy, bitter, spicy
Uses:	birth, menopause, insomnia; change, blessings, inner vision, prayer, transition and end-of-life care, dreams, clairvoyance, summer solstice, winter solstice, protection, letting go; enhancing healing powers, intuition
Properties:	balancing, relaxing, promotes sleep, anticonvulsant, very warming, revitalizing, opens the mind

domestic wild plant • culinary herb • traditionally used in Northern and Central Europe (North America, Asia) • foraging plant • can be burned without charcoal

Species of artemisia are found throughout the world, but mugwort is indigenous to parts of Asia, Africa, and Europe where it is important plant traditionally used for healing and in incense. Growing at the sides of paths and tracks, it was already being used for protection by the ancient Celts, its fragrance said to ward off evil spirits and imminent thunder storms, in addition to protecting against illness. At solstice celebrations, mugwort would be woven into a belt that would be thrown into the fire at the culmination of the ceremony to burn away negative energies and ask for protection for the year to come. Mugwort is used both as a herb in smudging and as a tea or infusion for women's issues and digestive problems. In smudging, it supports and accelerates childbirth and the expulsion of the placenta. It can also be used to bless a room and awaken clairvoyance. In China a species of *Artemisia* is used to make moxa cigars or sticks; when applied to acupuncture points, they are said to soothe a host of ailments. Prairie sage or white sage (*Artemisia ludoviciana*) is widespread across North America and Canada and is used in rituals and ceremonies.

Mugwort can also be burned as incense in the form of a smudge stick and is a useful ingredient of a smudging blend.

Myrrh

Name:	*Commiphora myrrha*
Family:	*Burseaceae*
Distribution:	Somalia, Ethiopia, Kenya, Saudi Arabia
Plant part:	resin
Scent:	perfumed, spicy, bitter
Uses:	meditation, divination; for inner peace, healing, success, happiness, contentment, cleansing, blessings, gratitude
Properties:	invigorating, revitalizing, grounding, calming, protective, disinfectant, anti-inflammatory, slows things down

traditional • Eastern • mentioned in the Bible

The *Commiphora* genus, which is found in the Arabian Peninsula, East Africa, and India, comprises a good 150 different species of myrrh. They all produce resins, however, some of which have been used as incense and remedies under various names since ancient times, including guggul, opoponax, and bdellium. Myrrh is one of the oldest known incense resins and is often mentioned in the Christian Bible, although it is uncertain whether it is the resin of *Commiphora myrrha* that is meant. In ancient Egypt myrrh was ritually burned at midday to honor the sun god Ra, and in Greece it featured in the smudging blend used by the Oracle of Delphi where it was part of the incense burned as an offering.

Myrrh is still in use today as a tincture for inflammation of the mouth and throat. It has healing and calming properties but should not be used to treat depression as it can intensify feelings of sadness. As a part of an incense blend, myrrh helps to harmonize the individual substances so that they work well together. It has a high melting point, so large pieces should be reduced in size (such as ground with a mortar and pestle) as otherwise it may not be possible to achieve the required temperature.

Myrtle

Name:	*Myrtus communis*
Family:	*Myrtaceae*
Distribution:	Mediterranean region, parts of the Middle East, southern parts of North America
Plant part:	leaves, tips of twigs, dried berries
Scent:	herbaceous, spicy, bitter
Uses:	fear, irritability; prayer, divination; harmony, cleansing, beauty, forgiveness, letting go, concentration
Properties:	balancing, bracing, soothes pain, opens the mind

mentioned in the Bible • important ancient incense • traditional in wedding decorations and bridal bouquets • also used as a spice and aromatic • related to the tea tree • popular house plant

Myrtle has been burned as incense since ancient times and is also mentioned in the Christian Bible. The Hebrews used it as a medicine and incorporated its branches into the construction of their tabernacles. Regalia for the dead was made from myrtle in Egypt, while in ancient Persia it was combined with bay leaves to make an incense used in rituals.

Myrtle was sacred to the Greek goddess of love Aphrodite and her Roman counterpart Venus, and it has traditionally been worn as a bridal decoration since ancient times, said to bring happiness and good luck in marriage. When burned in smudging, the smoke is said to soothe pain.

Nutmeg/Mace

Name:	*Myristica fragrans*
Family:	*Myristicaceae*
Distribution:	Maluku Islands, Borneo, Brazil, China, Thailand, Vietnam, India
Plant part:	seed, seed webbing (mace)
Scent:	aromatic, resinous, spicy
Uses:	depression, concentration; dreams; inspiration, visions, divination, clairvoyance, courage, energy
Properties:	stimulating, cheering, fortifies the nerves

spice • toxic in quantity

We are familiar with nutmeg as a spice that should be used in moderation due to its distinctive flavor that can soon overpower a dish. However, it is also important to take care over the quantity used as it is highly poisonous if too much is consumed; for example, one tablespoon of ground nutmeg or one whole nutmeg may be sufficient to cause problems. It should also be used with caution (and only in the tiniest quantities) when burned in smudging as it can cause headaches and nausea. Both the grated and the ground nut can be burned, as well as the mace (the webbing around the nut/seed). Nutmeg opens the third eye and makes us more receptive to visions. It is preferable to burn nutmeg over an essential oil diffuser as the scent can very quickly become bitter on charcoal.

Oak

Name:	*Quercus* spp.
Family:	*Fagaceae*, beech family
Distribution:	Eurasia, North Africa, North America
Plant part:	wood, bark, leaves
Scent:	woody, spicy, slightly pungent
Uses:	offerings, ceremonies of dedication; focus, cleansing, success
Properties:	antibacterial, styptic, anti-inflammatory, invigorating, grounding, clears the mind

domestic tree • foraging plant • sacred tree of the Celtic and Germanic peoples

The oak was a sacred tree for all the peoples of Europe and was dedicated to several deities: the Greek god Zeus, the Roman god Jupiter, and the Celtic thunder god Taranis (along with Donar, his Germanic counterpart). Celtic Druids would use the leaves of the oak in their cleansing rituals, while the bark in particular, which is rich in tannins, was used in herbal medicine to treat wounds and inflammation due to its antibacterial, styptic, and astringent properties. For smudging, it is preferable to use oak leaves in blends rather than as a sole ingredient, as they generate a powerfully pungent odor when burned alone.

Opoponax Myrrh

Name:	*Commiphora guidottii, Commiphora erythraea*
Family:	*Burseraceae*
Distribution:	Somalia and other parts of Northeastern Africa
Plant part:	resin
Scent:	spicy, sweetish
Uses:	anxiety, meditation, blessings; for protection, cleansing, grounding, transformation, partnership, intuition, balance
Properties:	grounding, balancing, relaxing, warming, mildly cleansing, brings a sense of security

Opoponax (also spelled opopanax and known as bisabolol) is a cousin of myrrh, and is sometimes also sold under the name sweet myrrh. Opoponax was originally the name given to the resin gum sourced from *Opoponax hispidus*, an umbellifer from the galbanum family, but this is no longer produced and the term is now used synonymously with opoponax myrrh. In its Somali homeland, an extract of the resin is traditionally used to bathe and disinfect the abdomen after childbirth or ritual circumcision, and it was also used to fumigate homes. When burned in smudging, it is said to sharpen our perceptive abilities, but it should always be used fresh, as it will otherwise lose its scent.

Palo Santo

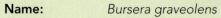

Name:	*Bursera graveolens*
Family:	*Burseraceae*
Distribution:	Mexico, Central & South America (Peru, Ecuador)
Plant part:	wood
Scent:	soothing
Uses:	muscle pain; meditation, sense of well-being
Properties:	balancing, centering, antidepressant, relaxing, antiseptic, anti-inflammatory

traditionally used in Central and South America • can be burned without charcoal

The heartwood of the South American *Bursera graveolens* tree is known as palo santo (meaning "holy wood"). It has been used in South America since the time of the Incas as an incense and oil for ritual and medicinal purposes. Palo santo was traditionally burned as incense to drive away evil spirits and to cleanse both the atmosphere and the participants of shamanic rituals. The wood contains so much resin that it can be burned without charcoal, and small shavings or spills can be lit directly and left to smolder.

The woods of various trees of the *Guaiacum* genus that are commercially available as guaiac or lignum vitae (meaning "wood of life") are also known as palo santo. Resins from other Central and South American species of *Bursera* are known as copal.

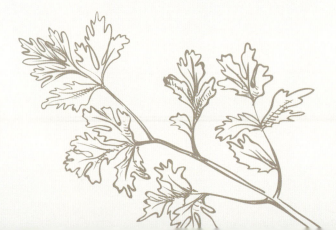

Patchouli

Name:	*Pogostemon cablin*
Family:	*Lamiaceae*
Distribution:	India, Philippines, Malaysia, Southern China, Vietnam
Plant part:	leaves
Scent:	woody, sultry, heavy, slightly earthy
Uses:	fear, meditation, concentration; love, aphrodisiac; insect repellent
Properties:	relaxing, calming, antidepressant, harmonious, grounding, aphrodisiac

Indian • popular incense

Indian patchouli (*Pogostemon cablin*) is associated with the hippy culture of the 1960s, when it achieved cult status as an essential oil and as a popular ingredient in incense sticks. It is still one of the best-known and most popular fragrances, with sensual, aphrodisiac properties. Patchouli is burned as incense in India to attract abundance and wealth, while an additional use is to place it among clothes to deter moths. Patchouli oil has been enjoyed for more than 1,500 years, and the best-known varieties come from India and Java. The plant is a distant relative of mint.

Peppermint/Mint

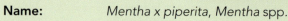

Name:	*Mentha x piperita, Mentha* spp.
Family:	*Lamiaceae*
Distribution:	Europe/Eurasia, North Africa, North America
Plant part:	leaves
Scent:	minty, herbaceous, earthy
Uses:	cleansing, healing; concentration, vitality, centering
Properties:	disinfectant, stimulating, energizing, clarity of thought

cultivated and garden plant • some varieties grow wild • well-known and popular

Peppermint originates in Southern Europe and, like so many other medicinal plants, found its way to the rest of Europe with the Romans and is now widespread in many parts of the world. The genus *Mentha* comprises many species, but most of the mint varieties we know today were only identified and recorded as such much later than the Roman era, with peppermint not being documented until the late 17th century. One of peppermint's most well-known uses is as a tea that is not only delicious but also effective against stomach disorders and nausea. Cooling and refreshing, mint tea is traditionally drunk in hot regions.

Mint has a mildly stimulating and antidepressant effect, purifies the air, and helps to clear the airways. As incense it was used by the ancient Greeks to revive someone who had fainted and to stimulate the mind. When burned in smudging, the various species of mint release very different scents.

Rose

- **Name:** *Rosa* spp.
- **Family:** *Rosaceae*
- **Distribution:** temperate zones worldwide
- **Plant part:** flower petals, buds
- **Scent:** floral, gentle, sensual, smooth
- **Uses:** meditation, prayer; against jealousy, for love
- **Properties:** relaxing for body and soul, cheering, opening up to generosity and kindness, harmonious, invigorating, heart-opening, sensual, blessings

domestic wild plant (dog rose) and garden plant • not all roses have a scent • traditionally used in the Arab world

Roses grow wild or are cultivated almost everywhere in the world. In ancient times they were associated with love and beauty and were a symbol of the goddess Venus. In Catholicism the rose is frequently a symbol of purity and love, linked with the Virgin Mary (rosary prayer). With its defensive thorns, the rose also represents protection, pain and sorrow, life and death. Roses are popular in bridal bouquets and funeral wreaths alike. When burned as incense, the smoke might be used to bless a house or for an evening of love, while in relationships of all kinds, it helps people to deal with disagreements with understanding and an open heart.

The buds of the Damask rose (*Rosa damascena*) are particularly fragrant, while the scents of wild roses such as the dog rose (*Rosa canina*), the field rose (*Rosa arvensis*), and the Western Wild Rose (*Rosa woodsii*) are also very intense. Rose petals and buds add an attractive dash of color to smudging blends.

Rosemary

Name:	*Rosmarinus officinalis*
Family:	*Lamiaceae*
Distribution:	Mediterranean region
Plant part:	leaves, tips of the shoots
Scent:	herbaceous, resinous, camphor-like
Uses:	parting, sorrow; blessings, opening the heart, harmony, letting go, contentment, protection, concentration, courage, creativity, inspiration, love, nature spirits
Properties:	comforting, stimulating, cleansing, antiseptic

traditional medicinal herb • Mediterranean culinary herb • known as "dew of the sea"

Deriving from the Latin *ros marinus*, meaning "dew of the sea," rosemary originated in the coastal regions of Southern Europe before spreading throughout the continent, where it first found its way into monastery kitchen gardens. Tea made with rosemary offers a good alternative to coffee as a morning drink thanks to its stimulating effects. It has similar properties to sage, and gargling or rinsing with rosemary water can be used to treat inflammation of the mouth and throat. Rosemary oil can help to soothe migraine and ease arthritic joints. When placed under the pillow, a sprig of rosemary is said to keep nightmares at bay and is a good addition to any smudging blend intended to promote sleep or dreams. The ancient Romans burned rosemary in honor of their household gods and ancestors. Rosemary is also said to stimulate and help with accepting change, and to support the process of parting and grieving. When burned as incense in smudging, it not only cleanses the air, its stimulating properties act on the mind, providing greater clarity and inspiration, and helping us to concentrate.

Sage

Name:	*Salvia officinalis*
Family:	*Lamiaceae*
Distribution:	Mediterranean region, parts of North America
Plant part:	leaves
Scent:	spicy, aromatic
Uses:	inflammation, gastrointestinal complaints, asthma; clarity
Properties:	powerfully cleansing, antiseptic, anti-inflammatory, reassuring, invigorating, energizing

wild Mediterranean culinary herb • garden plant • easily cultivated • can be burned without charcoal

Both common sage (*Salvia officinalis*) and white sage, its American cousin (*Salvia apiana*, see the page opposite), have been used medicinally and as incense since ancient times, and common sage was sacred to the Romans in particular. The name salvia derives from the Latin *salvare* (to heal), and sage was soon being grown in monastery gardens thanks to its healing properties. It was used to treat inflamed mucus membranes, gastrointestinal complaints, and coughs, but also to help reduce excess sweating. It was smoked in cigarette form to treat asthma or drunk as a tea, and bunches of sage were said to ward off evil spirits in the name of the Virgin Mary. Both types of sage can be burned as incense without using charcoal.

Sage (White)

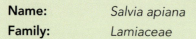

Name:	*Salvia apiana*
Family:	Lamiaceae
Distribution:	North America
Plant part:	leaves
Scent:	aromatic, resinous, herbaceous
Uses:	colds; rituals, blessings, cleansing, healing
Properties:	cleansing, calming

traditionally used in North America • can be burned without charcoal • used in smudge sticks

Like the European common or true sage (*Salvia officinalis*), this related species from the west coast of North America has been part of smudging and sacred rituals since time immemorial. Smudge sticks of white sage are used to cleanse houses and in ritual ceremonies, the smoke being said to bring peace and blessings, and the herb is also commonly used in the sweat lodge. White sage can also help to ease epileptic attacks and soothe colds and flu. It is not easy to cultivate, so most white sage is collected in the wild, but common sage and mugwort can be used as alternatives.

Sandalwood (Red)

Name:	*Pterocarpus santalinus* (also *Santalum rubrum*)
Family:	*Fabaceae*, papilionaceous plants
Distribution:	India
Plant part:	wood
Scent:	mildly spicy
Uses:	headaches; rituals, magic, blessings
Properties:	aphrodisiac

valued for its rich red color

Red sandalwood is not related to white sandalwood, and its scent is also less delicate and refined than the white, although more spicy. Red sandalwood is traditionally used externally, for example, as a paste applied to the forehead to treat headaches. The red variety is often included in smudging blends because of its attractive color and it is the principal ingredient in all red incense candles. Its magical properties tend to be based more on its color than on its scent.

Sandalwood (White)

Name:	*Santalum album, Santalum spicatum*
Family:	*Santalaceae*
Distribution:	India, parts of Australia
Plant part:	wood
Scent:	spicy, woody, sweet, warm
Uses:	insomnia, headaches, fever, skin conditions; meditation, transition rituals, evening smudging sessions; healing, protection, harmony, loyalty, cleansing, mental growth
Properties:	antispasmodic, expectorant, anti-inflammatory, relaxing, aphrodisiac

Eastern • popular • threatened with extinction

Most white sandalwood (*Santalum album*) comes from India, where it has a number of traditional uses. It forms an integral part of Ayurvedic, Chinese, and Tibetan medicine, used to treat headaches, fever, swelling, and skin conditions, among other disorders. It is also burned as incense at rituals such as weddings and funerals. White sandalwood's reputed abilities include the power to ward off evil spirits and free people from their sins, while in yoga and tantra, it is said to awaken the kundalini (an etheric force in humans described in tantric scripture) and calm the ego during meditation. Its fragrant wood is used to make ritual objects, murtis (icons), malas (prayer beads), and furniture. Sandalwood oil is considered an aphrodisiac because it contains substances similar to the male pheromone androstenol and the hormone testosterone.

White sandalwood is one of the most popular incense materials, but *Santalum album*, the plant from which it is sourced, is threatened with extinction and its export is strictly regulated. Due to high demand, sandalwood is not only illegally harvested and smuggled, but it is also faked. Australian *Santalum spicatum* may be of a lower quality, but it is an ethical alternative.

Scots Pine

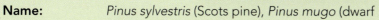

Name:	*Pinus sylvestris* (Scots pine), *Pinus mugo* (dwarf mountain pine), *Pinus cembra* (Swiss pine/stone pine)
Family:	Pinaceae
Distribution:	Europe
Plant part:	bark, resin, cones, needles, tips of the shoots
Scent:	soothing, warm, soft, resinous, woody
Uses:	respiratory conditions; protection, energy
Properties:	relaxing, calming, warming, invigorating, energizing, antiseptic, stimulates blood flow, strengthens the heart and lungs

traditional • used in soaps and bath products

Much like its cousin, the spruce, the Scots pine is one of the oldest sources of incense in the West. Although it is most common in the great evergreen forests of Northern Europe, the Scots pine can now be found on every continent and there is a practical use for almost every part of the tree. As a natural remedy, Scots pine resin helps to treat lung complaints, and it was used in incense to drive away evil spirits. The resin also has a calming effect, relaxing the nerves and bringing harmony to the mind and soul. A distillation process is used to remove the terpene oils from the resin, leaving behind rosin (colophony), a solid resin used on the bows of stringed instruments and by the electronics industry in flux for soldering. Scots pine is also used in soaps and bath products due to its antimicrobial properties.

Spikenard

Name:	*Nardostachys jatamansi, Aralia racemosa*
Family:	*Valerianaceae; Araliaceae*
Distribution:	Himalayas, North America
Plant part:	root
Scent:	earthy, musky, woody, spicy
Uses:	fear, unease, insomnia, stress; love
Properties:	powerfully balancing, calming, grounding, releases stubborn clinging energy

mentioned in the Bible • threatened with extinction • most spikenard today comes from North America • both species are traditionally used in rituals

Indian spikenard, the root of which can be burned as incense, grows in the uplands of the Himalayas and is known to have been used in temple incense blends and anointing oils in biblical times. The ancient world was aware that its smoke has a powerful sedative effect. Indian spikenard is now threatened with extinction, but American spikenard (*Aralia racemosa*) is grown in eastern parts of the United States, where it is also known as spice berry and petty morel, among other names. Something of a cure-all for Native Americans, it is used in a variety of rituals and for medicinal purposes. Although the two plants are unrelated, their properties are quite similar. Spikenard develops a pungent odor when burned as incense on its own, so it should primarily be used in blends; American spikenard should always be burned on a layer of sand.

Spruce

Name:	*Picea abies*
Family:	*Pinaceae*
Distribution:	northern hemisphere
Plant part:	wood, bark, cones, needles, tips of the shoots, resin
Scent:	spicy, powerful, green
Uses:	respiratory conditions, rheumatism; concentration, protection, inner peace
Properties:	disinfectant, grounding, cleansing, antiseptic, expectorant, clears the mind

domestic tree • traditional uses • foraging plant

Before frankincense became well known and affordable in the West, our ancestors would burn spruce resin as incense, earning it the name "forest frankincense." Spruce resin must be completely dry in order to be burned as incense, and although the burgundy resin available in pharmacies is a kind of spruce resin, it has also been refined and therefore does not have the same broad spectrum of properties. Burgundy resin has a more uplifting and invigorating effect, but it also generates more smoke. Smudging with spruce is said not only to remove disruptive influences, pathogens, and negative energies, but also to calm the mind. Together with juniper, spruce is one of the sacred incense plants used by Siberian shamans.

St John's Wort

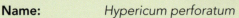

Name:	*Hypericum perforatum*
Family:	*Hypericaceae*
Distribution:	global
Plant part:	blossom
Scent:	very little scent of its own; slightly spicy, hay-like odor
Uses:	insomnia, banishing spirits; summer solstice, winter solstice, protection; cleansing the atmosphere, light-bringer, weather plant (sensitive to the atmosphere)
Properties:	antidepressant, mood-enhancing, calming, comforting, bolsters the nerves

domestic wild plant • ancient medicinal plant used for protection • foraging plant • for smudging blends

Said to have the power to cast out demons, St John's wort is a sacred plant in virtually all cultures. In Northern and Central Europe, where its bright yellow flowers are in bloom at the time of the summer solstice, it has been used since ancient times to ward off evil spirits and magical spells. The red oil extracted from its flowers is used to heal wounds and to soothe aching muscles, sciatica, and lumbago. It decorates altars on the feast day of the Assumption of Mary and forms part of the traditional herb bundles that are still gathered in Catholic areas and burned after mass, for example, to ward off the threat of storms. The effects of St John's wort against mild to moderate depression have now been medically proven.

Note St John's wort should not be used in combination with other antidepressant treatments unless under professional guidance, and it may interact with certain drugs. Before using St John's wort, consult your medical practitioner.

Styrax

Name:	*Styrax officinalis*
Family:	*Styracaeae; Hamamelidaceae*
Distribution:	Greece, Italy, Syria, Eastern Mediterranean
Plant part:	resin
Scent:	sweet, sensual, fragrant, floral
Uses:	insomnia; mental strength, love
Properties:	calming, relaxing, sensual, harmonious, opens the heart and promotes good mood

Eastern • in blends • used since antiquity

Originating in Mesopotamia, the styrax tree spread to the rest of the world in ancient times. The scent of styrax was ever present in ritual smudging on feast days in Mesopotamia and Egypt, and it was used as a fixative, much like ambergris (sourced from whales) in perfume, to give other scents longevity. Styrax was used medicinally to loosen phlegm and against bronchitis and other lung conditions, and also as a topical treatment for skin conditions and scabies. In addition to the classic styrax obtained from the styrax tree, so-called Asian and American styrax are also available, which are sourced from a variety of species of the liquidambar tree, another member of the *Hamamelidaceae* (witch hazel) family. Styrax is seldom sold in its pure form but is generally available as flakes or pieces of charcoal that have been soaked in liquid styrax balm. It should be burned only in small quantities and in blends.

Sweetgrass/ Vernal Grass

Name:	*Hierochloe odorata* (sweetgrass), *Anthoxanthum officinalis* (vernal grass)
Family:	*Poaceae*, sweetgrasses
Distribution:	Eurasia, North America
Plant part:	blades of grass
Scent:	sweet, warm, hay-like, vanilla
Uses:	colds, fever, pain; love, letting go; insect repellent
Properties:	antiseptic, blessings, heart-opening, relaxing, comforting, calming

traditionally used in many regions of the world • food ("bison grass") of the aurochs and/or buffalo • sacred for the indigenous tribes of North America • sweat lodge • peace pipe

This sweetly scented grass has a host of names but in the West is most often known as sweetgrass. It is native to Northwestern Europe and North America but has now become quite rare and its traditional uses would be in danger of being forgotten were it not for indigenous North American traditions. Its relatives, vernal grass and Alpine vernal grass, are commonly found throughout Eurasia and have similar properties and applications.

Sweetgrass provided nourishment for the aurochs (extinct ancestors of domestic cattle) and for the buffalo on the plains of North America. In Europe it was burned in honor of the goddess Freya and was also known as Mary's grass, as the Virgin Mary is said to have laid the infant Jesus on a bed of sweetgrass. It would therefore also be placed in the beds of new mothers and children, and also in those of the sick and the dying. It was believed to relax, comfort, and calm, while also offering protection against pathogens. Sweetgrass was scattered on Christian feast days such as Corpus Christi, and when placed under a pillow was reputed to awaken love and desire.

In Native American culture, sweetgrass was traditionally burned as incense and also smoked, and was used in many ceremonies, including sweat lodge and peace pipe rituals. It was said to put the participants in a relaxed and friendly mood, dispelling the negative energies of conflict and resentment. Today sweetgrass is woven into braids that are perfect for smudging as they can be lit easily without the use of charcoal. Sweetgrass is also taken as a tea to treat colds, fever, and pain, and the smoke can be inhaled to treat coughs.

Did you know? The sweet, hay-like smell of the grass comes from its coumarin content, which is also found in other plants and seeds, such as tonka beans. This can have an anticoagulant effect, so sweetgrass should not be used by people with blood-clotting disorders or who are taking anticoagulant medication.

Thyme

Name:	*Thymus vulgaris, Thymus serpyllum*
Family:	*Lamiaceae*
Distribution:	Europe
Plant part:	green parts, leaves
Scent:	intense, warm, herbaceous, aromatic
Uses:	colds and breathing problems, headaches; dreams, parting, nature spirits; self-confidence, cleansing, healing
Properties:	bracing, invigorating, antiseptic, antibacterial

Mediterranean culinary herb • garden plant • foraging plant

Thyme originates in the Mediterranean region and has a long history of use among the ancient Greeks and Romans, who would burn thyme as incense to keep away snakes and scorpions. It reached Northern Europe only much later, probably around the time that monastery gardens were being planted on the orders of Frankish king Charlemagne. Thyme is not only a versatile kitchen herb, it can also be used (with rosemary and sage) to treat colds and respiratory problems.

Thyme helps to soothe whooping cough, has expectorant properties in the treatment of bronchitis, and can also relieve headaches. When burned as incense, thyme strengthens the will and boosts vitality and self-confidence. Much like rosemary, it has a warming and revitalizing effect. When burned in smudging, the intense odor can be overpowering, so it should be used only sparingly in blends.

Tonka

Name:	*Dipteryx odorata*
Family:	*Fabaceae*, papilionaceous plants
Distribution:	parts of South America, West Africa
Plant part:	fruit
Scent:	sweet, vanilla, warm, herbaceous, hay-like
Uses:	serenity, harmony; insect repellent
Properties:	mood-enhancing, warming, balancing, sensual, relaxing, heart tonic

South American • use in small quantities (contains coumarin)

Tonka beans were carried as good luck charms in their South American homeland, but in the West they are known mainly as a spice. Due to their coumarin content, which is responsible for their hay-like odor, they should only be consumed (and smudged) in small quantities. The beans are ground or grated before use.

Verbena

Name:	*Verbena officinalis*
Family:	*Verbenaceae*
Distribution:	temperate zones worldwide
Plant part:	leaves
Scent:	bitter, herbaceous
Uses:	prophecy, clairvoyance, dreams, rituals, consecration, nights of Yuletide, summer solstice; concentration, self-confidence, courage, protection, blessing; sacrificial or weather plant (sensitive to atmospheric change)
Properties:	invigorating, centering, inspiring, energizing, aura-cleansing

traditionally used in Northern and Central Europe • domestic wild plant • ancient plant used in magic and as incense • often confused with lemon verbena, also known as lemon beebrush (*Aloysia triphylla, Aloysia citrodora*)

Verbena is a fairly commonplace perennial that has been valued for its properties in various cultures since ancient times. Known as the "tears of Isis" and "Hera's tears," verbena was popular not only among the Egyptians and Romans but also in particular with the Celts. It was a sacred herb for the Druids, who used it in divination and as a sacrificial plant in incense rituals. Verbena is also said to encourage prophetic dreams and to keep evil at bay. As a weather plant, it is sensitive to changes in the atmosphere, while in terms of an atmosphere between two people, it can help to dissolve tension. As verbena has no powerful scent of its own, it is a good candidate for use in blends.

Did you know? Verbena's relation, the fragrant lemon verbena, with which *Verbena officinalis* is often confused, is also effective when used in incense. It has a fresh, lemony scent that has a brightening and uplifting effect, and can help to calm anxiety, stimulating both mind and mood.

Vetiver

Name:	*Vetiveria zizanioides*
Family:	*Poaceae*, sweetgrasses
Distribution:	Asia, parts of North, South, & Central America
Plant part:	root
Scent:	earthy, heavy, sweet
Uses:	headaches, skin conditions, dementia, fever, snakebite; insect repellent
Properties:	aphrodisiac, bolsters the nerves

Asian incense plant • Ayurvedic • traditional burnt offering

Vetiver has many different uses in Indian and Ayurvedic medicine, including as a treatment for skin conditions, allergies, heart conditions, and dementia, but also for fever, malaria, and snakebites. As incense, it is combined with benzoin Siam resin and burned to ease headaches. It is also used in Hindu pujas (ritual sacrificial ceremonies), although in this case it is the leaves that are used, which have little scent, rather than the roots. In the West vetiver is used as an ingredient in men's cologne.

Yarrow

Name:	*Achillea millefolium*
Family:	*Asteraceae* (daisy family)
Distribution:	Eurasia, North America
Plant part:	flowers, leaves
Scent:	spicy
Uses:	menstrual complaints, gastric conditions, settles the nerves; dreams, visions, intuition, divination, nights of Yuletide, Candlemas
Properties:	balancing

domestic wild plant • foraging plant • herb bouquets • soldiers' woundwort

Yarrow is indigenous throughout Eurasia and North America. It was seen as the devil's plant in the Middle Ages, when allowing yarrow to grow in a garden meant running the risk of being accused of witchcraft, although at the same time it was also said to drive away the devil. Yarrow was traditionally used by Native American nations as an analgesic, among many other medicinal uses, including its ability to heal wounds and stop bleeding, a use to which it was also put in the American Civil War when it was called soldiers' woundwort.

Achillea derives from Achilles, the mythical ancient Greek hero, who is also said to have used it to treat wounds in battle. However, in German-speaking countries, its use focuses more on treating menstrual problems and related complaints. Yarrow can be made into a bitters tonic that helps with stomach complaints, and during outbreaks of the plague it was hung in bunches and burned to purify the air and to help protect against infection.

Yarrow is used for divination in many cultures. In China traditional I Ching sticks are made from yarrow stems. It is said to increase clairvoyance and to help protect on a mental and spiritual level, for example, by preventing bad dreams.

The wild plants, rather than the cultivated garden varieties, are more suitable for smudging. The smoke of yarrow burned as incense helps to bring balance to our lives. It also helps with dream work and the receiving of clear visions. Yarrow should be burned in blends or on a mesh.

Did you know? Yarrow is unusual in that it has certain contradictory properties—for example, it can help blood to clot but also stimulate bleeding (menstruation, nosebleeds).

Epilogue

THE BURNING OF INCENSE in smudging has a long tradition in all cultures, and though many of us have neglected the practice, we have not forgotten its lore. Just as the peace pipe is smoked in North America, incense is burned in the Catholic mass, and burning incense on charcoal accompanies prayer in every household in Greece, we too can once again make smudging rituals an integral part of our lives. If you are just beginning to take an interest in smudging, I hope this book has answered your questions, while if you already have a little experience, I hope it has inspired you to go further. It is my hope, therefore, that this book will take every reader a few steps further on their smudging journey.

Markus Schirner

About the Author

Markus Schirner has trained as a massage therapist and as a teacher in kinesiology, Brain Gym, and Touch for Health. His other specialist fields include aromatherapy, herbalism, meditation and breath therapy, and Buddhist philosophy. Schirner Verlag (www.schirner.com), founded by the author, is one of Germany's leading Mind, Body & Spirit publishers.

Picture Credits

Floral ornaments: artnLera; Initials: Madiwaso
Page: 5 matka_Wariatka; p. 6, 20, 127, 128: JurateBuiviene; p. 9: Bubbers BB; p. 10: Michaela Jilkova; p. 11: Esther Lin; p. 12: Pam Walker; p. 14 top: efoArt; p. 14 bottom, 28: New Africa; p. 15: Svitlyk; p. 22-23, 174-175: S. Birkelbach; p. 24 mikeledray; p. 26: J. Helgason; p. 36: Background All; p. 38: patpitchaya; p. 47: KieferPix; p. 48: Kuznetcov_Konstantin; p. 52: Olena Yakobchuk; p. 55: Lunar-Vogel; 56: Don Pablo; p. 57: Krakenimages.com; p. 61: irin-k; p. 65: G-Stock Studio; p. 66: Akarawut; p. 71: Vibe Images; p.72: schame, p. 73: dekazigzag; 77: Billion Photos; 82: Iryna Imago; 85: KieferPix; p. 88: thailand_becausewecan; p. 91: i7do; p. 92: Antonio Guillem; p. 94: Doucefleur; p. 95: Andrey_Popov; p. 96: TSN52; p. 97: Ground Picture; p. 100-101: Miriam Doerr Martin Frommherz; p. 102: larry.zhou; p. 103 in freedom we trust; p. 104: Katniss studio; p. 105: KarepaStock; p. 106: ThePremise; p. 107: ImpressionMall; p. 108: AmyLv; p. 109: 12photography; p. 110: M. Schuppich; p. 111: wasanajai; p. 112: mahirart; p. 113: Rifad; p. 114: islavicek; p. 115 top: hydra viridis; p. 115 bottom: George Trumpeter; p. 116: Yeti studio; p. 117 top: Quality Stock Arts; p. 117 bottom: Denis Moskvinov; p. 118: spline_x; p. 119: billysfam; 120: Natasha Sergeeva; 121: Madeleine Steinbach; p. 122: iva; 123: SakSa; p. 124, 133, 148, 165: Sarah Biesinger; p. 125: hjochen; p. 126: Heike Rau; p. 129: Halil ibrahim mescioglu; 131: ELAKSHI CREATIVE BUSINESS; p. 132: beta7; p. 134 top: sruilk; p. 134 bottom: Snezana Vasiljevic; p. 135: Melica; p. 136: Natasha Sergeeva; p. 137: FotoHelin; p. 138: AleMasche72; p. 139: LN Team; p. 140: a1vector; p. 141: Al.geba; p. 142: hande bagci; p. 143: liga_sveta; p. 144: LN Team; p. 145: Natalia Golubnycha; p. 146: avoferten; p. 147: vainilaychile; p. 149: Annmell_sun; p. 150: AYDO8; p. 151 bottom: Maxwell Photography; p. 152: KO-SIM; p. 153: Stephen Orsillo; p. 154: Sokor Space; p. 155: AB-7272; p. 156: Enes Solmaz; p. 157: efoArt; p. 158: Seyfettin Karagunduz; p. 159: Madeleine Steinbach; p. 160: Katniss studio; p. 161: Anton Starikov; p. 162: Kalcutta; p. 163: Ellen McKnight; p. 164: g215; p. 166: FooTToo; p. 167: Brent Hofacker; p. 168: Ingrid Balabanova; p. 169: 22Images Studio; p. 170: Titikul_B; p. 171: AmyLv; p. 172: 12photography; p. 173: Laustsen.

©Silja Bernspitz, Schirner: p. 130, 151 top
All others: shutterstock.com

Scan the QR code and save 25% at InnerTraditions.com. Browse over 2,000 titles on spirituality, the occult, ancient mysteries, new science, holistic health, and natural medicine.